The Formula of the Formulas

Alberto Uncini Manganelli

The formula of the formulas

From the sports champions, the inspiration
to bring out the best in ourselves

Foreword – Jose Mourinmho

THE FORMULA OF THE FORMULAS
Original title: La Formula delle Formule
Alberto Uncini Manganelli
First Italian edition: May 2025
First English edition: Novembre 2025

Drawings: Andrea Boschini
ISBN 978-2-9701538-3-2

All rights reserved

*I have always loved mathematics, analysis, equations.
I believed in logic and functions. I followed the numbers.
Only to then discover that what counts can never be counted.
A factor yes, but an intangible one. Unquantifiable. Indefinable.
The three of you
turn upside down the whole world I thought I understood,
beyond any logic, any measurement and any comprehension.
You are more than anything logical thought can understand.
You are all the reasons I could desire to exist.
You are my whole world and its every reason.*

ABOUT THE BOOK

22 world champions, 11 questions, 1 formula.

Countless insights on motivation, mindset, and the courage to give our best — because everything is possible, if we truly want it.

Winning matters. But more than that — wanting to win matters.

Whether in sport or in life, the will to give everything — to bring out our very best — defines who we are.

This book explores that spirit through the voices of 22 world champions, athletes and coaches whose extraordinary journeys reveal what it truly means to win. With a **foreword by José Mourinho**, it brings together perspectives from some of the most inspiring figures in world sport — from Olympic legends to football icons — showing how success is built through values, belief, and relentless determination.

Featuring: Tigist Assefa, Lance Brauman, Claudio Berardelli, Usain Bolt, Alessandro Del Piero, Sergio García, Natalia Goutlier, Grant Holloway, Peres Jepchirchir, Kaka, Jackie Joyner-Kersee, Noah Lyles, Roberto Mancini, Shaunae Miller-Uibo, Wayde van Niekerk, Ronaldinho, Arrigo Sacchi, Corey Seager, Stan Smith, Luiz Felipe Scolari, Ian Thorpe, and Xavi.

Is there a formula for achieving our best results — in sport and beyond? Yes. If we understand what success really is, what fuels our inner drive, and how willpower transforms talent into perseverance.

Talent, beyond talent.

In an era clouded by excuses and the acceptance of "average" as an answer, The Formula of the Formulas is a call to rediscover ambition — to value effort, resilience, and the desire to improve. Always. It reminds us that failures and setbacks shape champions as much as victories do. Passion and conviction are the forces that keep us moving forward, turning potential into achievement.

Because there is always a next step to take.

A new ball to kick,

A new point to play.

The Formula of the Formulas goes beyond sport — it's a manifesto for personal growth, coaching, and leadership, and a reminder that everything is possible when we give our best.

There is no limit.

Each copy contributes to programs supporting children's development through sport in underserved communities, via Common Goal (commongoal.org).

Inspired by the athletes, coaches, and stories that remind us why having the courage to give our best — and playing to win — truly matters.

Written by Alberto Uncini Manganelli — father, husband, and believer in sport, its values, and in the courage and conviction that drive the realization of human potential.

"Excellence is the result of caring more than others think is wise,
risking more than others think is safe,
dreaming more than others think is practical,
and expecting more than others think is possible"

"Excellence is the continuous commitment
to high quality performance
which produces exceptional results and value
that remains over time.
It's believing in continuous improvement and
in never being satisfied that something is less than
what it can truly be.
It's choosing the "best" as a lifestyle"

- Ronald Oldham – Claude T. Bissell -

We don't know a lot about Ronald "Ronnie" Oldham, he doesn't appear for sure in the list of titled champions. But maybe he was one.
After all, we need to first define who is a champion and why.
And we will try to do that.
Roland adapted this sentence from a quotation of Claude T. Bissel, Canadian author, teacher and eighth president of Toronto University.

FOREWORD

Jose Mourinho

Hunger to Win.

This is what defines a great champion.

I can't imagine that we, as coaches, should have to motivate an athlete to work harder or to be more ambitious. The desire to improve, to challenge oneself—this is already written in the DNA of top players. A true champion makes himself; no one creates him.

So, what is our role? Certainly, to put the player in the best possible conditions to express his full potential. To help him give his very best. I've had millionaire players whose careers were nearing the end, yet they showed an unwavering desire to win until their very last day. Others, despite immense potential, accomplished little because they lacked this decisive characteristic.

Unfortunately, today's society contributes to distorting reality, convincing some people that they can become true champions… without really being one. It's a widespread method of self protection, born from a culture that's become accustomed to making excuses. It's always wrong to generalize, so I'm not referring to all parents or all agents out there, but this tendency is evident. Without naming names, at Chelsea, I had a player whose father kept telling him, "As a midfielder, you have to score more goals, take shots from every position, train hard on long-range shooting." As an educator, the father was never satisfied. Well, his son ended up setting every possible record a Premier League midfielder could achieve.

Too many parents today, however, prefer to find excuses. My son isn't playing? It's the coach's fault, the tactical system's fault, the ball is too light, the shoes are uncomfortable… you see? It's never his fault. Never the player's. Ever. Maybe you're thinking of a similar situation with your own kids in school. They get a bad grade? It must be because the teacher didn't explain well enough. Didn't understand them.

But that's not how it works.

In sports, in life, anywhere.

This culture of overprotection can only cause harm, preventing young athletes from expressing their full potential. Today's footballer has two groups of people working with him: those inside the club and those outside it. And so, we end up with a private fitness coach who only focuses on him, a personal nutritionist who has to do something different from the club's nutritionist… contradictions arise easily, and this leads young players to find endless excuses to justify not reaching a high level of performance.

Just recently, after the transfer window had closed, I had a player who wanted to leave because the tactical system didn't suit him. But you see, that wasn't the real problem. The real issue was that he didn't want to adapt to the team—for a thousand distorted reasons. Instead of working hard and putting in the effort to integrate into a playing style, today, players prefer to go elsewhere, begging their agents to arrange a transfer.

So, what is our job as coaches, as educators, in the world of sports? And what should our own approach to success be? It truly pains me to see that we're living in an era where some coaches say, "I have my philosophy, and I won't change it." As long as you're winning, that mindset might be acceptable. But if you start losing, how can you still think that way? You're just building a wall around yourself—it's a self-defense strategy.

First and foremost, we are called to win titles. That's the truth.

And let's be clear: it wouldn't be fair to tell a coach or a team with limited potential that they must win titles. That's not the path for everyone. If, at the beginning of the season, the club sets survival in the league as the goal—if the owner, president, directors, coach, and players all agree on that target—then not being relegated is your "title." To say you've done well, you must achieve that goal.

Instead, people often hide behind their pride, clinging to their philosophy even when they fail to succeed, failing to meet the objectives set at the beginning of the journey.

That's not how you make history.

I want to close by going back to the first lines of this foreword, where I spoke about the mentality of a top player. These are the themes that Alberto explores in this book through the voices of those who have truly made history—on the field. In fact, on many different fields. And since I'm writing these words after a 3-0 Europa League victory, where the second goal was scored by Edin Džeko, I want to focus on him, hoping that many young players can learn from such an example.

On June 10, 2023, Edin played his last match for Inter—the Champions League final against Manchester City. Then, at 37 years old, he moved to Turkey. And you can imagine how many people thought, "He's just going there to make a lot of money, take it easy for two years, and then go back to Bosnia to enjoy life." Not at all.

Džeko came here and never missed a training session, never missed a game. He has always shown an incredible hunger to win, and I can even see it in small-sided training matches.

You're born with that kind of hunger.

And if it's real, if it's written in your genetic code, it never leaves you. It will define your entire career.

No psychologists, no external help. Of course, a coach can be a leader, a motivator—if he's good, he'll put you in the best possible conditions to give everything you have—but the most important thing is already inside you.

This is what it means to be truly rich: to have an insatiable hunger.

This is where the journey to success begins.

The rest of the path—you'll discover in the pages ahead.

José Mourinho

THANKS

A special thank you to those who inspired or helped the creation of this writing through a personal contribution.

Cinzia, Corrado, Francesco G., Maria, Max, Maxi, Paolo, Patrick, Ricki, Silvio, Stefano, Tom, for the time dedicated to the first reading and for the honesty of the first feedback which gave me the courage to continue and the inspiration to continue improving.

Thanks to Moritz for the indispensable help in the graphic exploration.

Thanks to Thomas and Riccardo for the English translation which I think reflects very well both the intent and the form desired by the author and by the champions.

Thanks to John, a true man of sport, for his precise and heartfelt editing of this English version — guided by genuine passion and a deep belief in the educational power of sport for the next generation.

Thanks to Luca who, first, believed in the book and created the conditions for its finalization and publication.

Thanks to Leonardo who, in the Italian version, accompanied me, in a surprising, stimulating and constructive way, and with feedback that was always clear and never obvious, in an editing process in which I think I learned a lot. Thank you.

A truly special thank you to all the champions who have decided to offer their contribution as an example and role model for each reader interested in how such extraordinary success in sport can be created, developed and motivated, with values, meanings and inspiration that transcend the discipline practiced and which can be interpreted in every field of application, including the professional one. Athletes of this calibre represent a model of behaviour and personal improvement for our lives. In the same way, sport is a teacher, I think, indispensable in every phase of our existence.

All the testimonies in this book were collected by the author in various and different interactions with the champions and translated from the original language trying to grasp at best their meaning.

COMMON GOAL

Every copy of this book contributes, via the donation of part of the author royalties, to projects that support the development of children through sport in underserved communities, powered by Common Goal. So that everyone can have access to sporting practices that have a decisive material impact on health, education and inspiring behaviour at each and every age.

Common Goal activates the power of football to bring people together and deliver positive, society-wide change.
As a football-focused network we work to connect the cultural and financial influence of the football industry with local organisations all around the world that use the beautiful game to dismantle inequalities and build a better future for all.
Our network works in more than 200 communities and over 90 countries to deliver change through football to young people. With decades of work in the field of football for good, we have seen that real, transformative impact is possible, through the shared joy that football brings.
It takes a team to win a game. This is why Common Goal works together with football institutions, private companies, governmental bodies and foundations, creating shared value and sustainable impact. Over the years, Common Goal has collaborated with more than 100 partners and allies the likes of adidas, Right to Dream and PepsiCo.
Common Goal also encourages professional players, managers, executives and clubs to donate a minimum of 1% of their salaries to promote and stimulate social change through football. Giorgio Chiellini, Vivianne Miedema, Dani Olmo, Naomi Girma, Jürgen Klopp and Casey Stoney are among the more than 200 professional players and managers who have teamed up with us.

TABLE OF CONTENTS

Foreword – Jose Mourinho	13
Acknowledgements	17
Common goal	19
Introduction	25
Why?	37
What is "winning"?	51
What's the formula of your success?	63
What were your major sacrifices?	75
Would you change something if you were to start all over today? Any regrets, missed opportunities?	
Who was the greatest influence on your career and your success?	89
What failures can you recall? What did they teach you?	99
Natural talent or hard work?	109
What is a winning mentality? Are there some specific qualities that are common to great champions?	123
Is it harder to win the first time? The second? Or to come back and win again?	139
Are more important the physical or mental strengths?	149

Do you have a ritual? Which one, and why?	159
If you had to give three pieces of advice to a young, talented athlete, what would they be?	167
The Formula of the Formulas: Conclusions	179
Bonus questions and answers: Sex or retreat? What's your biggest fear? Who is the champion of the century? If you would be another champion, who would you like to be	203
Athletes' biographies	218

"Success is not just a matter of how high you can go, but how far can you push yourself to get there. It is a journey of a thousand miles that begins with a single step and continues with a series of small, but determined, progressions"

- Unknown –

INTRODUCTION

I've always loved math.

Formulas and equations.

Data and facts.

A clear logic, undebatable conclusions.

Could I have provided you with a better assist to quit reading this book after just four lines?

Well, you know, I like to take risks.

I would understand if you stopped here, I really would. But if you've decided to put your trust in me, rest assured, I won't be lecturing you on quantum physics. Instead, we will talk about sport, champions, and values.

Let's be frank, mathematics isn't exactly a sexy topic, especially for someone who, for the entirety of his childhood, dreamed of becoming a footballer and winning the World Cup. I am referring to what we Italians call "calcio", with a rounded ball, whose spherical formula is much simpler than that of an oval ball. What's more, the other type of football, American football (which I adore), from what I can gather doesn't seem to have a World Championship. NFL athletes are labelled "world champions" when they win the Superbowl. And it's probably true.

But probably.

Not mathematically.

One thing is for sure: "foot + ball" is foot plus ball.

You play with your feet. There's no denying this. Mathematics is that set of rules that has always kept me glued to a sense of certainty.

One plus one is always two.

Mathematical.

Indisputable.

Above all, it's the same for everyone: honest, transparent, democratic.

And so, if you score, you can win. If you don't score, at the very best, you can draw.

If you don't shoot on target, you can't score, so you can't win. At most, you can draw.

Any objections?

More broadly, if you have the ball, you can use it, so you can score, and as a result, go on to win. Conversely, if you don't have the ball, you can't play it, you can't score, and therefore you can't even win, at best you can draw. After all, it was Pep Guardiola who, during his time at the helm of the legendary and all conquering Barcelona team, said "as long as we have possession, the others can't score." Self-evident, I would say.

This is mathematics, with its equations, its certainties.

Certainty equals justice. And this becomes even more important in our current world, where instead of having opinions based on facts, we have in front of our very eyes, tons of facts defined by opinions. Therefore, the perception becomes a reality accepted by everyone, as an effect of the social massification of individual opinions.

Everything is fluid, rapidly evolving, without a solid logical foundation.

Everything is true, therefore also the opposite.

And if everything is being judged, facts are at the mercy of opinions. Whoever makes the most noise, emerges victorious.

In the midst of such chaos, there's something nice in certainty, calculation, giving a clear form, sequential logic, that reveals without any fear of contradiction that by doing this… you get that.

A formula.

One.

Let's imagine that it can bring us success.

I belong to a generation that was brought up on teachings such as this one: the more you work your ass off, the more likely you are to do well and succeed in life. Simple, no?

I would say mathematical.

I don't consider it an ironclad rule. I don't maintain that it's the only possible way for all of us.

But that it's simple - mathematical, in fact - is something that we can all agree upon.

Run harder and faster than your opponent? You have a better chance of getting there first and winning back the ball. Work harder and better than your opponent? The odds of winning are on your side.

One more hour.

One more training session.

One more test.

One more try.

One more practice.

One more run.

And this is where the commitment, determination, believing beyond any doubt or fear, become crucial in making up for any difference in talent.

We're not all born with the left foot of Diego Armando Maradona or of Leo Messi. The less we have been blessed by genetics, the more we must work harder.

But even in the case of a natural talent, it is still a better idea to give our absolute all. Maybe, if that's the case, it will be a bit easier.

Maybe.

The aforementioned Argentinian star, 8 times Ballon D'Or, arrived for his first training session in Miami two hours before the rest of his teammates. After a two-decade long career, at unimaginable levels, he was still there showing everyone the value of hard work.

In just a few and unmistakable words, the message is the following: you must work your ass off.

Always.

Simple?

No, it isn't. For anyone.

Not even for someone born with that divine foot or with a DNA wired for success. You don't get anything by divine right.

It's the same in the professional world. You're chasing a promotion? It's not enough to perform extremely well at your current level. To show you can make the step up, you must prove that you can guarantee an excellent standard of performance worthy of the next level up. In short, show you can play at a top tier standard, even if you are currently in the second.

In sport, no one becomes the league's top scorer or winner of the European Golden Boot without having scored more than the others. This latter classification is so mathematical that it has specific coefficients for each championship, precisely defining the value of each goal depending on the tournament in which you score it in. In a world where opinions pull along the facts, here is an example in which without the facts - concrete and calculable - no award is given.

After all, at the Olympics, the one that stands on the highest step of the podium, in any discipline, is always the winner, not the one who thinks they are the best.

The two things can coincide, and the equation between winning and being the best can be true, but only with the result in hand. Facts shape opinions, and that's the way it should be. And facts also generate pure emotions (look at what is happening to tennis since Jannik Sinner started to win trophy after trophy).

There are no excuses. We are more than capable of avoiding problems and coming up with explanations, but the truth is the responsibility of missing out on a victory is ours alone.

No excuses. This was a concept I picked up from one of my bosses many years ago in Rome.

His words are still stuck in my head: "Don't explain!", he would say. Because there is always a good reason or an explanation for everything, but it won't change the result.

He was right.

A rule must be firmly in our minds right from the off, when we want to reach an objective: there is no shortcut for success, we always need to make sacrifices.

Blaming others, bad luck, or saying the stars simply didn't line up, won't get us anywhere. Instead, it's useful to convince ourselves that there is always something we can do. It is down to us.

It's a simple formula. It's not quantum physics. Purely objective data.

No turning away from the problem. No luck involved.

No divine right, no fast lane.

You must work hard; this is the only thing that will make the difference. Agassi became Agassi because he spent hour after hour squaring up and facing the constant bombardment of a tennis ball launcher. How many hours, how many more sacrifices compared to other tennis players, maybe with a better build, or with a better genetic predisposition?

More hours.

More training.

No guarantee of success.

Only commitment, to the very best of our abilities.

It's also a fairly clear way to show what really matters to us. The passion that burns within us.

Because where talent ends, we are spurred on by desire.

And where desire ends, only passion drives us on.

Think about how committed you were to a certain activity, when for you, it was nothing but a fun game.

Countless hours, as a child, spent playing football with Maxi and Ricki, until we were worn out, everywhere, inside or outside. Sure, all those hours didn't turn us into world champions (and who knows, maybe we deserved to, but that is another story… of three friends, one game!).

We couldn't count those hours, and yet, they counted. They meant the world to our friendship, shaping our set of values that made us what we are today.

Football was everything.

It was our entire world.

It was the rest of the universe that revolved around us.

No practice was "too much".

Play more. Learn more. Play better.

These were our rules. Simple. Shared. Mathematical, I would say.

Mathematics and sport teach us the importance of practice, perseverance and precision.

Just like every athlete relies on the hours of training to be increasingly competitive, every mathematician relies on formulas, obtained via trial after trial, error after error, to reveal the mysteries of the universe. In both disciplines, success is down to hard work, practice and passion. This is the only way to reach excellence.

And let's not forget to mention mathematics' sporting cousin, geometry. That set of rules capable of defining the trajectory of a majestic free kick, lifted over the wall, and sent soaring into the top corner. A piece of magic, don't you think?

Unfortunately, my knowledge of mathematics was far greater than my talent for football, which halted my route towards winning the World Cup. If it was a goal of mine, your honour, I admit I am guilty of failing.

In high school, to my surprise, I was won over by another subject: philosophy. It wasn't clear to me until I started getting very good grades, and nowhere near proportional to my studies. Maybe because it was to do with logic. I felt well-suited to the subject. Back then, my personal universe was made up of sport, mathematics and philosophy.

Oh, hang on, maybe four things: there was also Star Wars.

Thinking about it, Star Wars was nothing but a mixture of all three elements. Do you remember "The Force"? A unique, powerful energy that connects, unites and gives life to all things.

I don't know if you believe in it or not, but I do.

We believed. We didn't need to see to believe. On that subject, are wi-fi signals or radio waves visible?

The Force is something we cannot see and cannot explain in words, that perhaps we cannot fully comprehend at this moment in time… After all, try convincing the Ancient Romans to believe in the internet, Bluetooth or Zoom video calls. Go and tell the wise men from Ancient Greece, who coined for the first time the term "Philosophy" to air-drop photos taken during the Peloponnesian War from a thin tablet less than 10 centimetres long.

It's only a matter of time.

Sooner or later, we'll discover, study and use "The Force". I assure you.

Sport. Mathematics. Philosophy.

Sport: from the Old French "desport" meaning "free time" or "leisure". The oldest definition, from around 1.300 years before Christ, can be defined as "anything humans find entertaining".

Mathematics: from the Ancient Greek máthēma (μάθημα), which means "something learned", therefore also "study" and "science". The science of logic, quantity, structure, order and position. Many of its definitions refer to mathematics as the only, pure science. Mathematics involves counting, dividing food and territory, and keeping records. It has existed since the existence of man.

Philosophy: as previously stated, from the Ancient Greek "Philein" - "Sophia", "love, or loving, of wisdom and knowledge". Over time, it has also come to be known as the "meaning of things", whatever "thing" it is.

I won't ever be Socrates or Schopenhauer (and thank goodness…), but I like to think that even a classical subject like philosophy can be of value today in the search for deeper meaning. Without judgement or prejudice, without preconceived truths, but having the virtue of doubt, and curiosity.

Sport. Mathematics. Philosophy.

The joy of playing, the truth of what is irrefutable, the deeper meaning of things.

Joy. Truth. Meaning.

Only now, thirty years on from that fragile age and full of dreams, I understand their value, their bond and their "whys?".

And all my "whys?".

I have never sought anything more, better or different than that. I believe that there is a bond between them. In this belief that this bond exists, is there a formula that could be applied to sport, or better still, to success in sport as well as in our lives?

What if it were an inspiration to seek out and find your own path, whatever it may be?

To provide hope, meaning and value. As part of the research for this elixir, for this possible "formula of formulas", we asked a host of extraordinary talents from different sporting fields to answer a few questions.

Questions such as:

What is winning?

What is a winning mentality?

What matters most, talent or hard work?

What sacrifices did you make to reach your goal?

What mistakes or errors made you trip up?

Do you have remorse? Any regrets?

The aim was to produce a synthesis of common factors that can be applied to all, in sport or in other areas of life, to reach exceptional results.

I understand, it's an ambitious goal. But the fact that the "Formula of Formulas" isn't yet known does not mean it does not exist. Just like you can see the effects of the Force, without being able to comprehend them or analyse their nature. This is the reason why I have tried to define it, at least until others prove otherwise, naturally.

Of course, and this is a fact, many world class athletes have used their own winning strategy. So a formula exists, and the reason why lies in a simple and empirical observation: it worked. Those who made it work, were the best in their field, setting new records, writing history.

But be careful: we're talking about athletes, capable of singling out their own method and turning it into success, not robots. They are people that during their careers were troubled by the same set of doubts, the same form of inadequacy or inferiority, that we all struggle with. They had to take on the same obstacles, and deal with the same failures. They are ordinary people with the same demands, ambitions, and dreams. And the same uncertainties, doubts, and weaknesses.

Superhumans, perhaps.

But humans, nonetheless.

Following outstanding careers, they have developed their own point of view on success, what is needed to win, the strategy that has led them to write history and be a part of it, from now until the end of time.

The paths they took, and the choices they made, defined who they are, in what they believe, and the set of values that they today can pass onto the next generation. This mysterious mathematical synthesis comes from the spirit of sport, but it has a meaning destined to go beyond, to broaden itself to all aspects of our lives. Therefore, it applies to all of us, from the moment we have a dream to fulfil.

Our teammates in this journey have already experienced it, they have lived it in person, they have proved it.

It is the formula of the formulas.

"Success and failure are not measured by results alone, but by how much passion, dedication and commitment goes into playing to try to win. Because failure isn't being second or seventh or tenth, but it's about being second, seventh or tenth while accepting that you will not give everything to do the best you possibly can"

WHY?

I simply can't help it. I just like to know why.

That has always been the case for me: I find it hard to do something that I don't fully understand, or, anyway, I don't like it.

Because of that, I have a natural preference to ask myself, and others, "why?". Some of them understand the genuine nature of my curiosity, others don't and perceive it as a challenge to their own view or to their own proposals. In both cases I feel the need to know and understand the deeper meaning of things, before I accept "the thing as it is".

I have met people far more capable, accomplished and successful than myself who, when pitted against a certain situation, regardless of what it may be, rather than wondering "why?" to understand the underlying reasons and causes, they accept it as it is, answering that question with a simple "whatever, it's no big deal!". A more polite way of saying "who cares?".

What can I say? At the end of the day, they're probably right.

I mean, why bother trying to understand the meaning or the causes of an event that by no means we can change?

It is far more practical and convenient to accept it, and act based on the actual facts rather than investigating the reasons that brought about such a reality, which simply will not change, even if we were to identify the trigger. There's a specific wording that perfectly describes this kind of situation: coming to terms with it.

I too have somehow learnt to come to terms with it (while failing to understand the terms, which it pretty ironic). I can play along, if necessary.

In this path of personal learning, in the past, I have been lucky enough to observe first-hand and also learn a great deal from the success of people focusing on what rather than on why, capable of facing reality as it is, of grasping the tangible effects so as to exploit them and act swiftly and effectively, regardless of the genesis or the root causes. Their DNA must hold a gene that allows them to follow their intuition, with no need for a time-consuming search for the "whys" of things. By doing so, they quickly achieve extraordinary, fast and tangible results. Then again, perhaps their instinct leads them to results that aren't structural and are less sustainable in the long run and in terms of organisational growth (the intuition of one single individual cannot be replicated within an organisation).

This approach implies we should "push" people through precise tasks and actions, because those actions are defined from their own personal intuition and own intentionality, instead of "pulling" people towards a shared and collective vision, activating people's motivations towards a common objective and goal. Actions and results are often the result of contingent and short-term compromises too; there's nothing wrong about them, but they are linked to situational decisions and temporary contexts, not in a long-term perspective. And yet, they work. Indeed, without a short term, there's no long term, so why compromise or limit todays' success, for a future hope? I was lucky enough to learn a lot from this approach.

Also, in a very different way, I had the good fortune to witness the success of people focusing on why rather than on what, who had an innate need to understand things before taking action and to frame them within a bigger and broader picture, viewing it on the whole before judging or deciding something specific. These are people capable of leading and motivating others, even entire organisations, not heading for immediate goals but driven by the motivational strength of a mission, of an overarching and long-term view.

They don't push. They pull.

They need to appreciate the root causes of the problem to solve it structurally, definitively, or to be ready and aware should things go south again.

I was born amid the whys, with a more natural affinity to the latter approach. I can endlessly ask questions, owing to my instinctive, innate curiosity, and passionate need to understand the root causes and the reasons for what happens around me, and to act based on the comprehension, the general principles, and the overall picture. From the big picture to the detail, not vice-versa. I tend to dedicate sufficient time to explain to those who work with me why we do what we do, the reasons underpinning decision-making, so that all may replicate the basic idea and principles in new actions. In my opinion, that's how we can make everyone independent, based on a vision, on a goal, on a set of principles. Over time, I have adapted. I have become more selective when it comes to my whys, especially when I get the impression that the question is making the interlocutor uneasy. And I started to accept reality as it is, limiting the theoretical analysis, and facilitating the pragmatic action without questioning too much.

I have also learnt to let go.

Or at least, I try.

But why do I like to understand why things happen, the nature of human motivations, including the one that has driven me to write the book you're reading right now, and ask many questions to many champions, to better comprehend what their success conceals?

So... why? Why have I written this book?

Because I think we started telling ourselves about a big lie on the value and the meaning of winning and success (whether it's that of an individual or of a team).

We're telling ourselves that winning is not... winning. It's a whole lot of other good things.

And above all, that to hope to win it is not always necessary to give the best of ourselves.

And we are transferring this lie to the new generations, increasingly unable to orient themselves on what they really want, what they are searching for, how to achieve it, and consequently always dissatisfied with what they get.

We are getting confused about how to recognize success and defeat, and how to experience and digest them.

In doing so, the new generations receive the distorted message that winning is not... winning.

That success is not… success.

And that winning and being successful are not a direct consequence of giving your best, giving everything you have, every moment, every day. Always.

If winning no longer corresponds to ranking as number one, giving our best, putting in everything we can give, with the efforts, sacrifices and intensity necessary and indispensable to really try, then, in my opinion, we have a problem.

We are claiming that we are all above average (so how is the average calculated?), we tell ourselves that we are all good, and we convince ourselves that, in the end, there are many ways to realize oneself... or that it is enough to participate (a wrong interpretation of De Coubertin's words, we will talk about it later). That a certain negative result simply "must be accepted" as it is, that "you can't do better", and even that "you shouldn't get too stressed".

This is what I'm talking about.

Of the 'fact' that we shouldn't create unnecessary pressure on ourselves, because ultimately winning isn't everything. Just as not everything is the result of the math test the day before, perhaps because everyone else did poorly... so we are justified.

Or that we don't have to win a match to be a successful team, that we are worthy regardless of the commitment, or the continuous effort to improve our performances.

This attitude has harmful effects on work ethic, on maximizing one's potential, on managing defeat and, ultimately, on the ability to pursue self-realization.

The same thing goes in the professional sphere.

Everyone's good, everyone's part of a winning team.

But are we truly winning? Are we producing concrete results? If the answer is no, we need to acknowledge the unsuccessful outcome of our small or big missions and understand the causes of that failure. No matter how uncomfortable, unpopular and frustrating the cause underlying that failure may be, it's our only way to work on ourselves and improve.

I'm not saying that the search for fulfilment must not, or should not, be driven by motivations and goals other than the achievement of the best result. But that doesn't relieve us of our human and professional duty to give our very best in what we do.

Give the best. Give it all.

If we compete, we must do our best… We must give all we've got on the pitch, on the track, throughout the months of training and sacrifice that precede the game or the race.

Any given day.

Any given Sunday, as in the title of the famous movie.

Even when we study, we must do it to the best of our abilities. With curiosity, determination and commitment.

If we mediate, same. We apply discipline, consistency, care. We cannot just do it whenever we get the chance.

And we must do the same when we work, we must do our best: better than anyone else in our position, who has the same job, in the same role for the competitor in the same sector.

Or at least, we must try.

Always.

Not just today and then take a break tomorrow.

Always.

Winning is totalizing. It is for the best athletes, and we can observe exactly the same in successful entrepreneurs.

It starts with a personal commitment, consistent, persistent towards the continuous improvement and the search for excellence. It extends also to the personal sphere, to the point of striving for the very best in the daily and familiar activities, due to a natural curiosity, a constant pursuit of betterment and a limitless determination.

If we talk about sport, doing things is not enough.

If it's a race, entering it is not enough. A purpose is needed. A goal.

It doesn't matter whether it's about getting to the finish line or setting a specific time.

It's about yearning for something.

Trying to give the best we can.

Participating is not enough.

Defeat is not in losing, or in not winning, or in not achieving the goal, but it's in not trying the hardest.

We are talking about commitment, courage, hard work, desire. It's about aiming for the best possible result.

And there are no excuses.

And you know the good thing about it? Perhaps we won't make it. Our proper approach does not ensure the achievement of the result. And that's only fair, because it teaches us how to handle and deal with failure (a rather journalistic term, which great champions, such as Giannis Antetokounmpo have debunked and redefined), it spurs us to constantly improve, it ignites the emotions we need to feel, so that we can digest, manage and control them.

But if there is no victory and no defeat, intended as the extreme outcomes that can set you ablaze with joy or give you a nervous stomach that lasts for several days, how can we expect the new generations to deal with their feelings, to develop a solid work ethic, to discern what they deserve and what they don't and therefore aim for a constant improvement?

If failing to reach your goal doesn't eat away at your liver, can you really call it passion?

If the models followed by the new generations do not attach due value to commitment, to personal growth and to the sound and undeniable principle of having to work your ass off to reach any given goal, who will tell them that victory is not something you can just add to your Amazon cart? That it's not sufficient to add a filter to an Instagram story to make our path a winning one?

You know, sometimes the gap between seventh and first place is minimal, and it can be bridged. But that will happen only if we acknowledge the value of taking first place, without accepting a preconceived seventh place.

Seventh place is not defeat. Actually, seventh place can be highly successful per se, depending on the specific conditions of each path.

The real defeat is accepting that seventh place. Stifling desire, ambition, dreams... because... it's ok to be seventh.

We are defeated by self-limiting our dream, our aspiration and intention.

The defeat is limiting our will power.

That will, to overcome that extra hurdle.

That will, to make that extra sacrifice.

Basically, to earn that extra possibility.

Since when did we start telling our children that "it cannot be done"? That "it's too difficult"? That "it's not possible"?

Since when did we start telling our children that they can or should be satisfied with what they can give of themselves? Instead of encouraging them to try to do their best and take responsibility for their outcome?

Julio Velasco, one of the most admired sports educators and one of the best coaches in the history of volleyball, recently declared: "Today's young people are no different from the previous generations, but it is the parents who are different from previous generations." And then: "imagine a boy who has a problem at school, and his parents tell him that the problem is not him, but the teachers".

When did we start telling young people that giving your best is not essential?

That it's not worth trying or deluding yourself, because the possibilities are so few?

That any sufficient result will also be acceptable?

And since when did we start telling our kids that a fair amount of pressure is dangerous, instead of being a privilege for those with higher expectations and ambitions?

"Pressure is a privilege" is something Billie J. King, an icon in the history of tennis, once said. It's printed and enshrined – for future generations – in the corridor leading to the central court of Flushing Meadows, home of the US Open. That's right: pressure tells us what we're made of. When you apply pressure on something, it may break. There's a thin margin however… rather than breaking, it may actually compact and strengthen itself… like a snowball, made of compacted snowflakes, and its specific weight and impact is much greater than the snowflakes that formed it.

When did we start thinking that failing to make it is more penalising than trying and eventually failing? When did we attach more importance to the value of failing than the value of trying?

Tom Brady, one of the greatest quarterbacks in the history of American football – claimed by many to be the greatest of all time – went straight to the point:

"To be successful at anything, the truth is that you don't have to be special. You just must be what most people aren't. Consistent, determined, and willing to work for it".

That's right. We are not defeated by a lack of talent, rather by the lack of consistency, determination and work ethic. By the lack of expectations and aspirations.

And that's exactly the risk that new generations, which have plenty of talent, are facing.

So, let's ask ourselves: have we explained to our children that talent alone will lead you nowhere, or that even if you don't have an outstanding talent everything is possible for those who truly believe it, who are truly driven by passion and can rely on an unwavering determination and will?

I don't know how, but things must have played out like this: at some point, we started thinking that working hard, truly believing in it and always being consistent over time did not represent the foundations of education, in sports and in life. And yet, winning should be a constant goal, not just a temporary, random or fleeting one.

When we were kids, we used to love heroes, because they would prevail in the clash between good and evil.

Good would defeat evil.

Actually, it would triumph.

The concept of victory has always been clear. Crystal clear.

Mathematical.

1-0.

1st.

It has always been enshrined in our way of assessing the results of any competition.

And also, in how we weather the lesser challenges of adolescence. For example, when we used to play football during breaktime, Year 2 versus Year 3… we would leave scraps of knee skin on the asphalt of Piazza Trento Trieste… Because no superficial injury could be worth the pride we felt for the following 24 hours for winning the game, or the great frustration from losing it.

We must not get confused: the meaning of defeat has always been clear. And that's no longer the case now. Since when does losing no longer mean… losing?

Sure, if we don't appreciate the value and the role of victory, it's going to be very difficult to picture the function and meaning of defeat.

That's why sport is extraordinarily important: it gets us used, day by day, to winning, losing, sometimes drawing; to process the emotions and treasure the lessons that such results bring about; it always makes us want to try, to have courage, to give everything we can, and to learn. Bottom line: we feel the need to become better athletes and better people. And all of this happens with every single hit, every single pass, every single day, every single training session, every single match, because "On any given Sunday you're gonna win or you're gonna lose. The point is – can you win or lose like a man?". In the film, Al Pacino was speaking in the men's changing room, but the concept obviously goes for all of humanity, called upon to win or lose, but with dignity.

Above all, sport teaches us to turn the page.

That's right. Because being able to get up on your feet again is a precious attribute, typical of great champions. It's a talent that can surely be innate, in some individuals, yet it's something that can also be learnt, when our organism, our being, knows how to process a defeat because it has trained properly and it has learnt to produce the enzymes required to digest it, as well as the platelets that seal the scars. Quickly. Before the damage becomes chronic.

Turning the page is a skill that we can train. It's within our reach. Provided that we do not just settle for it. Provided that we do not lower the bar to ground level, so that it's easy to get over.

Because even when you're playing a Wimbledon final, every single point is and must always be the paramount thing. But once the point is won or lost, it's in the past. From that moment onwards, only the following point matters.

The following point, the following match, the following challenge.

The lessons of the past will give us confidence, inspiration, and once archived only the next ball will count. And then it will be our will to multiply our forces to try to win a new, exciting challenge. We find all these ingredients in the thoughts of our champions, who have already written history, and together with them we will try to derive the formula.

The formula of the formulas.

"Winning isn't everything, it's the only thing.
It's not something occasional
It's a habit
It's an attitude
It's a way of living".

- Vince Lombardi -

WHAT IS "WINNING"?

What is winning?

What is winning…

…easy: being first.

In a game, a race, a test, an exam, an election, achieving or exceeding a pre-defined goal.

An absolute winner is also number one.

It's sheer mathematics.

Number 1.

Many could say all the rest is just a lot of talk.

As a matter of fact, victory has spanned across generations and cultures, taking on very different forms, interpretations and meanings.

Even more so today: the meaning of victory is evolving and reshaping as the new generations, Z and Alpha, are growing.

Generations born in an on-demand world, where everything responds to and is obtained with a movement of your finger. Literally.

These generations have a different approach to victory and have an alternative interpretation of success, through a set of values that are very distant from the ones we were used to. When I say we, I mean generation X and – to a certain extent – the Millennials too.

Here is the problem: you can control and command TV, social media, tablets and apps… but you cannot do that with life.

You cannot command victory.

You cannot command success.

Quite frustrating, isn't it?

There's no button, no app.

It's not for sale, nor on-demand.

We cannot just order a winning mentality, nor the result of that winning... mentality. At least for the time being, until we'll be able to distil a winning mentality and channel it into a touch device.

We'll come back to this later, when we'll ask our champions about the working your ass off concept, which has been reworded into a softer title on sacrifices. But for now, let us assume that in an on-demand world, where everything is at hand, winning is not just a button you can press, a command to be performed.

And thank God for that.

But let's go back to our dear mathematics.

As we said earlier, winning = number 1.

That's it, mathematically speaking.

But leaving figures aside, what is winning about?

Is it about the intensity of the path to be followed?

Is it just about being the first to cross the finish line?

Is it both things?

"Why?" my teenage daughter would ask (I wonder who she took after ...)

Is it about the race? Or the preparation?

Is it the result of talent? Or of hard work?

Is it the effect of an indescribable passion? Or of an irrational obsession?

Or both?

Is it the result of crazy perseverance and of the determination to constantly strive for excellence?

Does it derive from the boldness of trying?

From the ambition of making it?

Or from the folly of beating all statistics?

Assuming that mathematics isn't actually everything (man, it's hard for me to write this, my hand is trembling!), several meanings can be attached to winning, depending on the context. Yes, it is often connected with performance, strategy, ability or luck being greater than those of your rivals. However, victory could also represent a subjective concept and vary according to individual goals and to the definitions of success. Indeed, several philosophies that have developed throughout the centuries in different regions of the world seemingly provide different interpretations of victory.

From the standpoint of existentialism – associated with many European philosophers of the 19th and 20th centuries and deeply rooted in the exploration of meaning, purpose and worth of human existence – victory is to be seen in the creation of one's own purpose and meaning in life, in terms of very personal and individual results. It's therefore about taking the reins of your fate, affirming your liberty, while acknowledging that we are individually responsible for shaping our future.

From a Nihilist point of view, winning would be pretty different, probably having the opposite meaning. In this case, winning would be arbitrary, meaningless and potentially useless, given the premise that life has no true meaning, no practical sense, no specific purpose. To the point that winning would often be a fleeting distraction from the sensation of an existential void. Or even an artificial creation of the mind, with no real or intrinsic value.

Utilitarianism, on the other hand – which basically tends to maximise benefit and utility, the only two elements that can really define overall happiness and wellbeing for the vast majority of mankind – would assess victory based on the positive impact it has in boosting happiness and reducing suffering, for oneself and for the others affected by the consequences of actions.

In the context of virtue ethics, typical of Greek aretaic beginning with Socrates (no, not Sócrates, the Brazilian footballer, but the philosopher himself!), the focus shifts to the nature of each individual (regardless of the actions or consequences), hence the definition of winning would rely on the nurturing and exercise of virtuous behaviour, namely, equity, courage, determination, perseverance. Victory would therefore be the manifestation of individual personality traits, a demonstration of human excellence.

The very concept of winning would change yet again in Oriental philosophy (such as Taoism and Buddhism), where victory would find its truth in personal balance (with oneself and with the elements), inner peace and general holistic harmony. It's more a matter of being aligned with a natural and somehow predetermined order of the universe than actually prevailing. This meaning would be nurtured by awareness, leaving aside material desires and without bothering too much about the results.

All of this is apparently what winning means.

Apparently.

One single term and so many and diverse dimensions, depending on cultures and philosophical outlook, but also on generational gaps.

On the whole, this word has a multifaceted philosophical meaning, which can be interpreted in different ways, depending on one's personal set of values. It can include aspects related to personal fulfilment, to social utility, to moral excellence, to existential accomplishment or to spiritual enlightenment, among others.

Now, all that said and done… is this what winning is about?

Is there a bit of all of this in it?

Something of all of this?

It's time to ask those who have really won. Multiple times.

All of their extraordinary biographies are summarized in few words at the end, and even if a few simple words cannot give justice to their achievement, we will learn in the next chapters how they got there.

What is winning?

USAIN BOLT
Winning can mean different things to different people. For some, winning is being happy in life. For others, winning is reaching your objectives.

RONALDINHO
The reward for a life of sacrifices, effort and dedication.

PERES JEPCHIRCHIR
Winning for me means having success in life.

LANCE BRAUMAN
It's trying your absolute hardest and giving your best performance in the most important moment.

GRANT HOLLOWAY
Crossing the line first, but also succeeding in something you want to achieve, whether it be a short- or long-term goal.

WAYDE VAN NIEKERK
Winning is growth. I've never been focused on winning in the grand scheme of things, I've always focused on growth, the moment and being the best version possible of myself. And with this obviously comes the desire to then win and the desire to improve. Once you have tasted victory, you always want it. So, my objective has always been to grow, but after that, the objective has been to win, because that is where my standard can be found.

NATLIA GUITLER
Winning is knowing there is still a long road ahead, which in turn prepares you for that moment. It's knowing that you have to be

dedicated and give up a lot to reach the highest step of the podium, but in the end, it will be worth it.

XAVI

When it comes to football, winning is the end goal for me. It's the reason we work so hard each week and, in the end, it's the reward for a lot of teamwork and effort.

KAKÀ

The concept of winning changes a lot in each stage of our life. When we are young, we think a lot about victory as success. With age, winning becomes more about looking back and seeing that you have left a good legacy in everything that you have put your effort and heart into. Today, the family that I have built and our rapport with God, are the biggest sense of success that I have.

TIGIST ASSEFA

Winning means fulfilling my target. It's not only about crossing the finish line first but about achieving the goal I set for myself and giving my best performance.

STAN SMITH

It's about making the most of your potential, whatever it may be. You can't do any better than try to unleash 100% of your potential. I have the utmost respect for those athletes that come close to fulfilling their potential but aren't necessarily the best in the world. They are the ones that have less talent but have worked really hard in order to come close to fulfilling their potential.

CLAUDIO BERARDELLI

For me, winning should represent just one step in a much broader journey of personal growth. I believe that winning as a coach goes beyond the personal gratification of being successful. Perhaps it's the awareness of having contributed not only to the athletic but above all to the personal and human growth of the athletes you coach. Something far more lasting than victory itself.

FELIPE SCOLARI

Winning is reaching the goal you have set out. It is about reaching a specific objective.

JACKIE JOYNER-KERSEE

Winning means showing total commitment to a task, working hard every day to obtain the best results possible and performing to the best of your abilities.

IAN THORPE

Being able to walk away knowing that there was nothing else you could have done to be the best on that day or in that moment.

ROBERTO MANCINI

Winning is everything. It's the ultimate objective in sport, and you must do everything possible even if there aren't the means to do so, but you always set out to win. You have to give everything. You may not make it happen, but if you have given everything in order to win, then you have done your job.

ARRIGO SACCHI

Winning is honouring the people that have trust and belief in you. It's also important to be deserving winners, because a win that is not deserved, is not a victory. Being worthy winners means dominating the game, and always being optimistic, because without optimism there is no desire to improve, and without the desire to improve, there is no winning mentality. If you want to be a hero, you have to give it your all.

SERGIO GARCIA FERNÀNDEZ
Winning is the satisfaction of seeing all your hard work fully pay off.

COREY SEAGER
Winning is simply winning. Being the best. Reaching the top of the mountain.

As you can see, the relationship between great champions and victory in sports often features three major areas:
Effort. Dedication. Sacrifice. You can achieve anything. You must be prepared to give it all. To reach your full potential.
Preparation. Growth. The endless process that makes us constantly better and fulfils our potential. It requires commitment, consistency and perseverance. There's no end to constant improvement.
Excellent performance at the right time. There's a right time and place for everything. Delivering a top performance in the most important race or match really makes the difference.

According to the above, it seems that winning is essentially much more than outperforming the others.
Sure, it is revealed by measuring a result, but it is truly achieved through the constant, incessant realisation of one's own potential. Perseverance, effort and the tireless search for excellence represent the victory of human spirit over obstacles and adversities. It shows the power of determination, the ability to overcome challenges. Whether it's external, personal or material goals.

We think we fight for victory, but by doing so we dig deep into our inner strengths, searching for the determination and resilience that raise the bar of our expectations. Or shatter them.

Winning testifies to our courage, our dedication, our confidence in ourselves and in the people who, in turn, believe in us.

It's not just about the result, rankings or medals. It's not just an objective. And it's not just about reaching the apex of success. It's about the journey, the lessons learnt, the growth experienced along the path. It's about setting ambitious goals, that can truly inspire us and compel us to pursue greatness, even when pitted against limits, failure and setbacks, so as to leave a long-lasting legacy.

This is how we learn that, as we search for victory, what we really discovery is our inner strength, our will and our potential – exploited or unexploited. In this journey that leads us to discover our inner selves, to growth and to change, we pave our way towards excellence, powered by a dream that is fulfilled through an infinite, irrational and sometimes insane passion.

Based on the experiences of champions, as we walk the path that leads to discovery, we are strongly aware of the specific, tangible and measurable goal. But passion, enthusiasm, the constant and limitless search for excellence go well beyond all mathematical formulae, ushering in a world of meanings that make that number 1 a vaster universe, where there are dynamics dictated by logic and motivations fostered by deeper feelings, which we cannot command, which pierce the human soul and elude our grasp.

Champions are shaped through adversity by working hard, boasting an unwavering conviction and self-confidence.

They are ignited by passion.

Determination.

And courage.

*"Success is the result of doing things
other people will never do
to get where other people will never get."*

- Unknown -

WHAT'S THE FORMULA OF YOUR SUCCESS?

Natural born talent, training, constant commitment, discipline, mental strength, physical strength, resolve, resilience, concentration, personal convictions, coaching quality, body management, learning, continuous improvement, intrinsic motivation, adaptability to different circumstances... The most successful athletes are the ones capable of integrating all of the above elements in their path. They are all crucial factors. So, what is it that makes a tangible difference?

Let's mathematically assess a one-year growth path of two athletes, who start on a par in terms of talent and enhance their performances with a difference of just one percentage point per day.

Let us simplify this to the max:

If A does 100 push-ups today, B does 101, then 102 the following day, and so on.

If A runs 100 minutes, B runs 101, then 102 the following day, and so on.

If A takes 100 shots on goal, B takes 101...

Every day, B advances by one percentage point compared to A, and every day B adds that extra 1% compared to the previous day (this also goes for the teenager who calculates one extra equation in 100 compared to the classmate... it's something that can be applied to any type of exercise).

And that's the pattern for each factor that can be measured, shaped or improved through training and exercise. After one year, the difference can be seen in the graph below... a factor advantage of 40. That means 40 times as much!

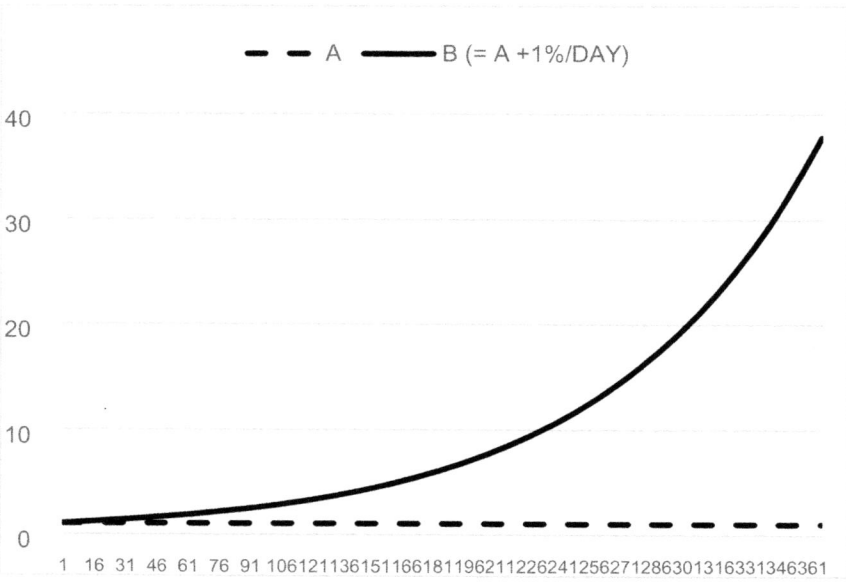

This is clearly an extreme case but let us look at the figures: in such a comparison, one of the two athletes creates the conditions for a 40-fold improvement, every year.

For those who prefer formulas to graphs.... it is as simple as this:

$1.00 \wedge 365 = 1.00$

$1.01 \wedge 365 = 37.78$

Almost 40 times! Not a bit more, but a 40x difference.

Very small differences each day, make a huge gap over time. Again, and again, those differences compound, creating a significant difference that materializes in raised chances of success, 40x, physical and skill development, 40x, up to the full difference between winning and losing, being number 1, or not.

That is pretty impressive. In terms of chances of success – given the same starting level of talent – the difference is remarkable, even for one single year.

Now let's multiply that by a 20-year career.

Let's opt for a more typical case: suppose that every day, an athlete performs just one more exercise than the other athlete (if one does 10 push-ups, the other does 11; if one runs 10 minutes, the other runs 11; if one takes 10 shots, the other takes 11.). That will be the constant difference. So, unlike the previous case, there's no daily increase. It's just that constant, daily extra exercise.

After one whole year, a very slight daily difference (one extra repetition in ten, you can distinguish the line right below) will turn out to be worth more than a month's training (365 repetitions, divided by the 10 reps per day rule means 36.5 days of training...)! In a 20-year career, a difference that apparently seems so minimal corresponds to almost two extra years of training!

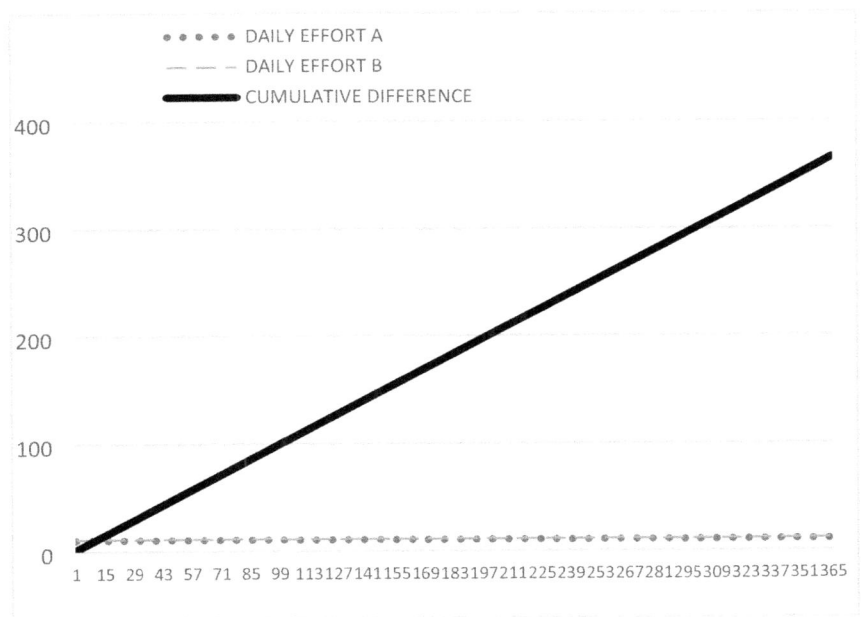

This is where will, dedication and consistency come into play: a little extra effort, every single day, really makes the difference.

Something that might seem insignificant in that very moment turns into a huge gap or an unreachable edge after only one year.

Let alone after twenty.

That's what mathematics tells us.

It's unquestionable.

It's just like that.

Sometimes I'm asked, "how do you find the time to write books, given that you're always so busy?"

Well, let's suppose I write half a page a day, every day, and that it takes me about 20 minutes.

It seems doable. It's not a huge effort.

Over a one-year period, I will have written a 180-page book, including the covers!

Doing that little.

Very little.

Constantly.

Every time.

It's what we add up in the end that makes the final sum.

But this thing about determination, consistency, daily marginal extra efforts that generate huge gaps or edges after several months or years is just one of the aspects of the game. It's just one of the factors that enables potential talent to produce successful results.

A factor in the formula.

USAIN BOLT

My formula for success is the combination of talent, hard work and discipline. I was born with the talent to run fast. I had a lot of success from an early age without too much training. When I reached the professional ranks, I realized that everyone had talent; therefore, hard work became necessary to reach the top. To be great, you need concentration and discipline.

ALESSANDRO DEL PIERO
It varies from one individual to another. For me, it's a combination of dedication, learning from failures and continuous improvement. In three words: perseverance, learning, improvement.

RONALDINHO
Perseverance, humility, enjoyment.

PERES JEPCHIRCHIR
Hard work, patience and never be afraid.

LANCE BRAUMAN
The formula for my success, as a coach, is turning up to work every day and showing total commitment. In three words: discipline, responsibility and character.

NOAH LYLES
Teamwork, ambition, willingness to learn.

GRANT HOLLOWAY
Practice makes things permanent, and permanent things become history. By reaching your objective with consistency each time you take to the track, you are able to prolong and make success permanent.

WAYDE VAN NIEKERK
Perseverance, sacrifice and hard work.

NATALIA GUITLER
Dedication, perseverance, resilience.

SHAUNAE MILLER-UIBO
Faith, love and hard work. I think it's important first of all to love what you do. When you love your work, it seems less difficult and therefore working hard also becomes enjoyable. What makes it all that much easier is my faith in God, knowing he is the one that gave me this talent and that he will be alongside me every step of the way.

XAVI
Work, perseverance, never stop believing in yourself.

KAKÁ
Concentration: I've always tried to concentrate on every goal I had without distractions. Dedication: I've always dedicated myself to what was important to me, in both my career and with my family. Faith: without faith and without union with God, nothing in my life would make sense.

TIGIST ASSEFA
Hard work, patience, and discipline. These three values guide me every day in training and competition.

STAN SMITH
You start with talent. You need a large dose of talent to be at the top level, while good coaching is important to give continuity to your technique and type of game, creating a solid base to build on. Then it's crucial to train with a specific aim. If you really want to become good quickly, every time you hit the ball you should have a purpose in mind. Every single time. Where to direct the ball, the rhythm you hit it with,

and then the spin. Finally, it's vital to also have a good attitude during the whole process while always remaining positive: you could be a great player, even a professional, and not win a tournament. You lose every week. And so, you need to have a good perspective of what it means. In three words: talent, commitment and perspective.

CLAUDIO BERARDELLI

I've asked myself that many times in over twenty years in this profession — and honestly, I sometimes wonder how I've managed to stay at this level for so long, considering all the challenges that high-performance sport brings. Probably there's only one reason: every single day, whether it's a good or a bad one, I try to show up. Maybe sometimes at the expense of my personal life, but I've turned my work into a sort of personal mission. "Showing up" — always and no matter what — has probably made the difference.

FELIPE SCOLARI

Discipline, dedication and team unity.

JACKIE JOYNER-KERSEE

There is no single formula. It definitely requires commitment, hard work, a determined attitude, the ability to never stop demanding the best from yourself both mentally and physically.

IAN THORPE

Always be yourself as a person and always aspire to be better. Aspiration, inspiration and integrity.

ROBERTO MANCINI

The commitment, the perseverance and the desire to make it, going onto achieve things considered impossible.

ARRIGO SACCHI

First of all, you have to really love what you do. You need passion. You must accept just one certainty: that is, you can always do more, and you can always improve. And never betray those that believed in you. I always looked for humble players, reliable, intelligent and polite. People, before players, those that put the club ahead of the team and the team ahead of the individual. People that loved what they were doing and that had a huge amount of desire to continuously improve. People that never felt like they had made it and were not soloists or individuals.

SERGIO GARCIA FERNÀNDEZ

Talent. Hard work. And believing in yourself.

COREY SEACGER

Dedication, preparation, execution.

So, let's formulate.

Talent + Passion and Belief + Constant disciplined hard work + Winning mentality + Continuous improvement = Success in sports.

Talent is a starting point, never the final one. It can be decisive, especially at first, but never sufficient in the long run, when facing many opponents with a similar mindset. If pure talent does not go hand in hand with other factors, it cannot ensure success. We have seen countless youngsters with a great potential, who have never made it to the top because they lacked will, dedication, discipline and humbleness, all which factor into an equation that cannot be fragmented while hoping the same result may be achieved.

Passion and joy for what you do, along with strong belief, can drive and shape talent, making it long-lasting. The belief may be religious or sheerly personal. Basic talent and DNA can construct a rocket that is technically perfect and if it is then fuelled with the cutting-edge propellent of passion and self-confidence, it will reach supersonic speeds. It will travel far, almost reaching the stars... unless it explodes.

Yes, because talent and passion alone can make you explode or quickly burn out.

That's why constant, disciplined work must come into play to continuously refine technique, strengthen the body, cleanse the mind... in order to always be on top of your game. When you're driving at 300 km/h, when you're running the 100m sprint in less than 10 seconds, you can instantly burn out months of work. One single kick of the ball can change an entire season, hence the margin for error is extremely narrow. One centimetre, one second, or both, can make the difference between winning and losing. For you, but also for your team.

That's quite something, isn't it?

Unique talents, driven by great passion, must still work hard and strive for excellence, and then go for it, gaining that extra centimetre or second.

If you want to be on top you need a mindset that aims to overcome all challenges, in all circumstances or conditions, despite any obstacle, so that you may reach your goals... and there are no excuses. When conviction, attitude and behaviour come together they drive a person to do their best and retain confidence and determination even in the most adverse situations.

It's not just the determination in the moment that makes the difference. It's also a humility-driven attitude: never rest on your laurels, always try to continuously improve. That's what great champions do. They constantly think about bettering themselves.

Every moment. Every day.

There is no nine-to-five, or five days a week, if you want to improve.

There are no smart work hours.

There is no Zoom or Teams.

Excellence has no working schedule. You cannot just turn it off, it has no switch.

And no timer.

You cannot click it. It doesn't even have a touch screen.

It's a choice. Connected to our expectations of ourselves, to the quality standards of our actions. A choice that is reflected in the expectations we have of the world around us.

It is not born from a specific moment. It's a way of thinking.

Of acting.

And of living.

"If we are not willing to sacrifice the usual, we will have to be satisfied with the ordinary".

- Jim Rohn -

"Working hard for something you don't like, it's called stress.
Working hard for something you love, It's called passion."

- Unknown -

WHAT WERE YOUR MAJOR SACRIFICES? WOULD YOU CHANGE SOMETHING IF YOU WERE TO START ALL OVER TODAY? ANY REGRETS, MISSED OPPORTUNITIES?

Starting all over from scratch after a successful career may sound punishing. Put simply, for the regular person it means getting a new opportunity to tackle the past armed with the learnings taken from the future. It's like going back to the starting line with plenty of extra cards to play.

It's like doing an already-solved assignment in class.

Or playing again a match, you've already seen.

And yet, following a successful story, how can we think we can change the factors of a perfect formula? It is said that you don't change a winning team.

But every story leaves in its wake a whole raft of sacrifices, compromises and, sometimes, regrets. Victories are often the result of painful choices; in the specific context and moment they were taken. It's been that way for all sporting legends. And for us, common mortals.

How much is the desire for the future worth, compared to the enjoyment of the present?

What are you willing to lose, in order to stake on the value of your ambition?

What scars to be healed are hidden behind our choices?

USAIN BOLT

I don't think I would do much differently. I had a good career, but looking back, I would have liked having run the 200 meters in under 19 seconds, which was possible had I prioritized it, and it would have been out of reach for the next generation of athletes. During my career, I always tried to have a good balance between work and enjoyment. For me, it was always important to enjoy myself and I did better when I had fun. Of course, there were sacrifices, but looking back, there weren't any sacrifices that weighed me down.

ALESSANDRO DEL PIERO

The biggest sacrifices were free time, relationships with others and sometimes health. Balancing career ambitions with my personal life was the most demanding aspect. If I were to start over again, I would focus more on my mental health. I would first find someone who could be a mentor during the whole process, and I would certainly balance my work and personal life more effectively. There were missed opportunities, but I try to learn from them rather than have regrets. Each one was a lesson on how to make better decisions in the future.

RONALDINHO

The tough days of training right from a young age and the sacrifices associated with being away from friends and family for long periods took their toll. Even if football is always about joy and positivity. It's hard to say, but I don't think I would do anything differently. In our life, there will always be failures and successes. I am grateful and happy with everything that I have achieved. Having done something differently, would not necessarily have been a guarantee of achieving more. Life is made up of choices, some right and some wrong. If we look back, we will always find things that could have been done better or differently, but nothing that causes any sense of regret.

PERES JEPCHIRCHIR

I make sacrifices by working even harder in training. This is what saw me achieve what I did in my life. My biggest regret is the 2024 Paris Olympics. I didn't expect to finish 15th, because I prepared well and expected to do well. I was disappointed how it went because of an illness I was recovering from, and I couldn't defend my gold medal from the previous Olympics.

LANCE BRAUMAN

The biggest sacrifice for me is the amount of time I have spent and still spend away from home and the impact that has on my family life. Their understanding and acceptance motivate me even more to have success. If I were to start all over again, I honestly wouldn't change much. All my experiences have made me into the coach I am today.

NOAH LYLES

There have been lots of sacrifices, and sacrifices are part of our job. If you seriously want to be the best you need a lot of dedication, concentration and healthy habits. I have a set program for everything, and I am intent on avoiding bad habits. In the end, it becomes the norm to say no to parties, weddings, holidays, meeting up with friends, if you are in the middle of preparing for an important event. It almost doesn't cross your mind because you have been doing it for so long, but when you can't be at the wedding of your best friend then these are big sacrifices. I wouldn't change anything at this moment, and I don't think I have made any major mistakes. Any injury I had was always short and well handled, and we always pulled out of every race in which we thought we would get injured. And we have had lots of success: we've won a medal in every big championship I have taken part in, so I don't think I would change a thing.

GRANT HOLLOWAY

Excluding myself from my group of friends was a big sacrifice. They would go out, have fun, and party. Meanwhile, I always tried to find space to concentrate on my dream of becoming Olympic champion. However, I wouldn't change a thing, the victories, the defeats and the sacrifices are what made me who I am today, and I would not swap my journey for anything.

WAYDE VAN NIEKERK

I think most of my sacrifices were quite fulfilling and paid off later in life. It was definitely tough and demanding to travel far away from friends and family. But seeing how I was able to make everybody proud, and the contribution I made to help us live a better life, and the things I achieved in the end, has been very satisfying. So, all the sacrifices paid off. My biggest regret was my injury in 2018 (rupturing my cruciate ligament playing rugby with family and friends). From 2018 to today, I would have been able to achieve a lot of things and victories and enjoy lots of opportunities to challenge myself to the fullest. I would have been able to explore and find the best version of myself and get the most out of my sport. But because of a wrong choice, which caused me a nasty injury, it changed my career which became one of continuous recovery, a fight to get back to the top and become stronger.

NATALIA GUITLER

I remember that when I was 16, I had to choose between becoming a professional tennis player and my studies. I decided on a tennis career in Argentina, which meant I had to give up everything I had in Brazil (family and friends) to follow my dream! Without doubt, it was one of the most demanding moments I have ever experienced and a massive sacrifice. If I were to go back, I would certainly work better on my psychology. I would train and strengthen my mind better for all the situations that an athlete has to face. My biggest regret was when, at the age of 16, I had to choose between playing and studying in the United States or embarking on a professional career. Maybe today I would choose differently, going to the United States to study, play and then try to make it as a professional starting from there.

SHAUNAE MILLER-UIBO

I think that making sacrifices makes success even sweeter. It keeps you even more grounded and disciplined, not only in sport, but it also allows you to achieve something even bigger in life. I wouldn't change a thing. Throughout my career, I have had so many setbacks that have turned into experiences that I have learnt from, and without them, I would not be the person or athlete that I am today.

XAVI

Perhaps the biggest sacrifice has been that, to reach my objective of becoming an elite athlete, I lost out on some of my youth by not being able to do things that my friends or people my age did because I had to take care of myself and lead a disciplined life. But in the end, when I look back and take stock, I think that what I achieved goes well beyond anything I had to give up. As I have always said, I had a career that I could not have even dreamed of, so I don't think I would change anything. I have no regrets.

KAKÁ

The career of a professional athlete is made up of sacrifices from the start to the end, and even when it is over. If you want any chance of making it to the top, your dedication has to be extreme. I have made lots of physical sacrifices, psychological and even family ones to get to where I am. The burden comes with the enormous responsibility of being at your best; loads of fans and people, family members and friends that start to count on you. This is perhaps the biggest burden we encounter. Having always been very focused and dedicated to all the goals I set, I don't have many regrets. We are not perfect beings, and even if I could start all over again, I would have my faults, and this is normal. If I were to start playing again today, I would have a personal physiotherapist that would accompany me. But there is nothing I regret. At times, I think about how it could have been had I made different choices, it's only normal. In life, you can't follow all the opportunities that come your way. Naturally, I made choices that opened a certain path and automatically took me away from other routes that I could have followed.

TIGIST ASSEFA

My biggest sacrifice has been time—especially the years I could have spent starting my own family and having children. But I believe I still have time for that in the future, so I don't have regrets.

STAN SMITH

I couldn't do any other activities or sports that I would have liked to do, such as basketball, during my high school career. I gave it up during the season in my final year. It was a pretty big sacrifice. I would have liked to have played with our high school basketball team because we had a great team and, seeing as we reached the semifinals of our tournament in South California, it would have been fun to be in that team. I also missed out on parties and high school social activities; I didn't do many of those things. Even in college, I trained, played or had tournaments constantly. But looking back, I was truly blessed with what happened in my life, apart from an elbow injury which I really regret not having sorted out sooner. I think I should have stopped for a bit and let it heal, but I kept on playing and in the end, I had to have an operation a couple of years later. If I were to play today, I would have a coach, a fitness coach, who would work with me daily to help me avoid injuries and make decisions in a precautionary manner.

CLAUDIO BERARDELLI

I don't like to talk about sacrifices, because I still feel privileged. I do a job that isn't really a job — it's an integral part of my life. Passion, yes, but also more than that. That said, I sometimes look back and wonder who I would be, and what I would be doing, if I hadn't left home at 23 to begin an adventure in Africa alongside some of the greatest runners in the world. I can't deny that as a young man, I lived a rather unconventional life, giving up a normal social life — something I still miss today. There's always something one would change from the past, but that gives me the strength to think about how to move forward better in the future. Regrets? Many... but I carry them with me as part of my journey as an individual in constant evolution.

FELIPE SCOLARI

In the career of all those who work in football, the biggest sacrifice is being away from family during special and commemorative dates. Not being with your children and seeing how they are growing up is definitely very difficult to deal with. However, I would not do anything differently. I studied, was dedicated, made mistakes, learned and got results. I remember before the 2006 World Cup in Germany, during my time as Portugal coach, I was asked to become manager of the English national team. They wanted to set up a meeting to agree on a contract before the World Cup. I said no, and that I would only discuss it after the World Cup, because it would not have been ethical and fair on my part. The conversation ended there, and they didn't contact me again. But I don't regret it. I did the right thing.

IAN THORPE

I missed out on a lot during my childhood. My friends did different things, and I trained 30 - 40 hours a week, but on the flip side, it was my choice. Not to mention everything that I earned in comparison. I had an extraordinary life that I continue to live today and that I also enjoyed in that moment. I don't know if I would change much, in reality I am very pleased with the success that I have had, but also of the experiences that have made me become the person I am today. I have no regrets. Perhaps the only chance I missed out on was when I had the opportunity to beat the world record in 2002 in the 400 meters front crawl. It was a race in which I didn't swim at full speed, but I didn't have any idea that I was that close to the record. I could have swam faster.

ROBERTO MANCINI

There were lots of sacrifices: I left home when I was not even 14. I left my family, friends. This changed my childhood. I had to grow up quickly. The sacrifices were enormous, but they also paid off. I would do it all again. In my day, it was very different. When you are young, sometimes you don't always make the right choices, or you don't always give everything you have. Yes, when I was younger, I could have worked harder. I think that we all have opportunities in life or missed opportunities. But overall, I think it's part and parcel of life. When you must make choices, at times you get it right, at times you get it wrong.

ARRIGO SACCHI

The time dedicated to family is the biggest sacrifice. I lived football in an all-encompassing manner. I could not ask the players to give their all and their best if I was not the first one to do so. For me, football is like a film, you can't improvise and it's all written. Take Brad Pitt, who follows a specific script. You need a lot of preparation, work, and study.

And you experience it all as one. You attack in 11 and defend in 11, you all work together. I had to sacrifice a lot of family life.

SERGIO GARCIA FERNÀNDEZ
The biggest sacrifice was not being able to dedicate enough time to family and friends having to travel so much. I would not change anything, because all the experiences I had helped me to learn and grow both as a player and a man.

    If handled well and with a correct, optimistic and positive outlook, sacrifices and regret are an integral part of all processes concerning growth and personal fulfilment. Usually, every sacrifice implies giving up an immediate personal reward in favour of a greater result, in the long run.

    So, everything boils down to a matter of priority and perspective. For youths especially, but also for anyone who mainly focuses on the contingent aspect of things as being all and now, or carpe diem, it's very unlikely that something intangible, uncertain and "future" could prevail over the most immediate, rewarding and gratifying choice. That's exactly where motivations, ambitions and priorities step in, as well as strong personal beliefs.

    It's not a matter of doing the right or wrong thing, it's a matter of preferring either the short or long run, the tangible or the intangible, concreteness or a dream. The two options don't necessarily rule one another out, but they might do over time. Furthermore, you cannot sacrifice everything, sure, but it's also not reasonable or plausible not to sacrifice anything if you want to achieve something, and better results.

    So how do we decide?

    What are we willing to sacrifice, that is currently a certainty, in exchange for an unguaranteed expectation tomorrow?

When mathematics or statistics don't provide a real solution to the equation sacrifice vs. success (and the opportunities it provides) our only option seems to be a leap of faith.

We cannot calculate the statistical probability of success of an athlete based on the number of parties they will have to miss out on in high school... even though common sense tells us that preserving one's energies for training and for the race makes it somewhat more probable to train or play better.

And this is where philosophy intervenes, intended as the propensity to attach a more profound meaning to what we do (rather than just doing it), which goes with hope, a concept similar to faith, for example: when we behave aptly in life, hoping to get to a heaven that nobody has ever seen.

What a mess!

It all seems to be very complicated.

But in the end, how important is that party compared to the result in the following day's game?

What is our awareness of ourselves, our priorities, our goals?

And of our dreams?

What's the value of a dream?

Do we wish to let go of a dream, albeit one that might be hard to fulfil, in exchange for an extra party that is surely happening now?

We're talking about parties, but there's also precious time to be dedicated to family. Leaving one's hometown and loved ones takes away a lot of that time.

What are we willing to sacrifice, then?

The answer cannot be nothing. For that means that our goals will be worth nothing. If the answer is everything, then that dream truly is worth everything to us.

The problem lies somewhere in between, since there are no mathematical laws that quantify the value of the dream versus the burden of sacrifice.

There is no probability calculation that can give us some reasonable feedback.

The awareness of this decision-making comes from our inner selves.

Either you feel it, or you don't feel it.

If, on the path to success, nothing is worth nothing, then everything has a price, nothing is certain and nothing is obtained by right, in a world where greatness takes... everything (that was the beautiful slogan celebrating Nadal's retirement) how much of what is certain are we willing to lose... in order to win – with no certainty of it?

The only certainty is the importance and value of one's own desires, along with one's willpower.

It's the attitude of aspiring beyond all expectations.

Believing beyond any probability, beyond any doubts.

Wanting it, beyond any reason.

"The people who influence our path are the ones who pushed us to see beyond our limits, and to believe in our dreams".

WHO WAS THE GREATEST INFLUENCE ON YOUR CAREER AND YOUR SUCCESS?

Having a mentor is not optional. Even world-class champions need it. Having support in inspiration, in growth, in the assessment of challenges and opportunities can make a great difference, especially in the most delicate moments, when we are more fragile as we face an increasingly competitive world, where there's no room for believing that luck can be a solution.

Being able to rely on a compass, someone who guides you in a specific direction, who is objective and keeps a proper distance, can help you gain confidence, handle uncertainties and find inner strength, motivation and encouragement to overcome the most critical phases with great resolve.

At the onset of a career, the foremost sources of inspiration, support and motivation are your family and your first coaches, but over time a wider and more outlined team is formed, consisting of many other people who might affect your choices and provide a broader support.

Many champions found in their parents, or one of the two, the driver capable of pushing, guiding or inspiring them during the initial phase of their journey. There is always a "primus movens" (in Latin first mover), someone who managed to spot your talent, supported it, protected and developed it, ever since day one. No doubt about that.

I would say mathematical.

Many others perhaps could never rely on the same kind of support, and this might have been a crucial factor in terms of their path and final result. Perhaps we'll never know.

So, who was the first to spot our talent and skills?

Who plucked up our courage when we were facing weaknesses that are common to all, including great champions (when they were at the very start of their careers)?

Who gave us hope amid difficulties and converted doubts into fuel for growth?

USAIN BOLT

I think it's important that the motivation comes from within, but it's always nice to have a good team behind you. I give a lot of credit to my coach Glen Mills for my success on the track because he found a way to make me train intensely without getting injured, which was the key to my success.

RONALDINHO

My brother Roberto. From a young age he took on the responsibility of protecting me, giving up a lot of things in his personal and professional life so I could become what I am.

PERES JEPCHIRCHIR

My brother is the person that supported and encouraged me, and he was an important figure in my path towards success.

LANCE BRAUMAN

My love for this sport started when I was young thanks to my father (who is also an athletics coach). Nevertheless, wanting to see my athletes reach their highest level is what drives and pushes me to try to be the best I can be.

NOAH LYLES

My mother played a key role in my success. My whole family, brother, sister, mother and even my father, gave me good genes. What's more, my team is decisive in everything. My agent, my chiropractor, my masseur, my therapist… a team that keeps me responsible and allows me to have a soft landing in every circumstance. My mother probably had the biggest impact on my sporting career, but both my parents had a big impact. My father was my first coach and introduced us to the world of track and field, from world championships to Olympics, and he got us excited about the idea of performing, looking at data and getting to know the history of this sport. My mother showed me essentially how to take your dream and turn it into reality, making sure you keep the right people around you to keep on growing.

GRANT HOLLOWAY

I've always tried to lead my life by being on the driver's side, trying to steer myself towards my objectives. I have a wonderful family that supports me in everything and a team that allows me to train and continuously improve.

NATALIA GUTLIER

My father has always been very influential when it came to becoming a tennis player, and from a very young age, I started playing racquetball and then tennis. I have three older brothers who always played football, and they let me play with them ever since I was little; so, they were all very responsible for my career as an athlete.

SHAUNAE MILLER-UIBO

There are lots of people in my life that I thank for helping me along the way towards my success, but my mother and father have always been at the top of that list. They made a lot of sacrifices right from the start so

I could do what I love. They motivated me and inspired me every day to be the best that I could be. And I will always be grateful because I have been blessed with two parents that believed in my dream and wanted to see me have success. My parents, my husband, my family, they have all played a significant role in my career. Helping the people by your side, whether things go well or not, is very important to me. I help people that I can always rely upon, that I know have my best interests at heart and that I know want to see me have success. They are a huge part of my motivation and reason why I have been able to have so much success in my career.

XAVI

In the order in which they entered my life, I would say the three people that influenced my career the most are my father, Joaquim, because right from a young age he knew how to guide me in life and in football. Joan Vilá, who was the first to help me understand the game, and Luis Aragonés, who was perhaps the first coach to give me the required confidence to get the best out of myself.

KAKÁ

My biggest role model was always my father, for the integrity he always showed, for his calmness in making decisions, for his respect towards others, for his family values and for always keeping me in touch with reality even when I was at the top.

TIGIST ASSEFA

In my life, my mother has influenced me the most—she taught me to be strong and to work hard. In athletics, Tirunesh Dibaba has been a big inspiration and influenced me greatly.

STAN SMITH

There are a certain number of people, certainly my parents had a good outlook. They weren't those types of parents that spent all their time with you. They supported everything I did and when they really got to know tennis, I was already out on the tour. Also, my brother always encouraged me and this gave me confidence. A person that really made a big difference was Pancho Segura: one of the best coaches of all time at the highest level. He worked with Connors and Chang and other players, and he helped me with the mental side of the game. Then George Toley, my coach in college and Dennis Ralston.

CLAUDIO BERARDELLI

My family definitely played a key role in my African adventure. Leaving home at 23 to live so far away, in a country so culturally different from Italy, was surely a test for them. But they never asked me to give up or consider an alternative. My father always pushed me to believe in what I was doing. Unfortunately, I never really had a true mentor — someone to call in difficult times (my father was that figure, but not for the technical side of my work). However, I owe a lot to all the athletes I've worked with over the years. They, more than anyone else, have helped me grow and become the coach I am today.

FELIPE SCOLARI

When we start our career, we always need a teacher who shows us and teaches us. As an athlete, I had a teacher in Caxias do Rio Grande do Sul, Carlos Froner, who showed me the importance of discipline, dedication and how to manage a group.

ROBERTO MANCINI

My career was influenced by my father who pushed me when I was a child. He had a lot of belief in me. He always thought I could become a footballer. He took me, without anyone really knowing, to Bologna when I was 13 and before I was even 14, I had moved from Jesi to Bologna. And then there were the various coaches and the experiences that shaped me along the way.

ARRIGO SACCHI
The librarian in Fusignano, a village of 8 thousand people, where I lived as a child, Alfredo Belletti. He was the one that got me into football. When I was 19 years old, I played two games in the fourth tier and then Pivatelli stopped playing me. So, I decided to go and work in a factory and that's where I stayed for seven years. Then Alfredo, who was also an Italian and Latin teacher, asked me to play in the second tier. I played that year, and we stayed up. But because of a bad back I told Alfredo that I would stop at the end of the season. At that point he said "Well, in that case, you can coach". He also told me that I could build success with ideas and work. I was not sure about the ideas… but work yes, that is something I knew about, so I got the team to train every night for a month. In the first match we beat the league favourites 2 - 0. That's where my journey started. It was, however, quite a rare event because my starts have always been complicated, even if I have never been fired.

SERGIO GARCIA FERNÀNDEZ
My parents, and especially my father who was the first to teach me how to play golf.

COREY SEAGER
My wife Mady. She stayed by my side in the difficult moments and in the best ones. She pushed me to be the person I am away from the pitch, which means that I have become a better version of myself out on the pitch. She has been my steady rock who has helped me move forward and always pushed me to be better.

A guide that is a source of inspiration, protection and support is not someone you can always haphazardly bump into.

Sure, some have found it at home, in the most natural (and appropriate, I may add) way, if I can make some sort of theoretical assessment.

But let us not assume that it's a right granted to you at birth. It is actually very important to search among those closest to us, such as parents, teachers, coaches. Ask them for some proactive advice. Observe people a lot and identify someone you can admire and from whom you can constantly learn. From the best teammates in your team to other colleagues in the professional sphere, it is critical to look around and observe anyone who embodies the values, the skills and the attitude that may inspire your path.

We can always learn from everyone.

We must be curious, ask questions, never take anything for granted.

To take fate into our own hands, showing willingness to be humble, learning and improving consistently.

The most successful people I have met have created, developed and retained very close relations with at least one mentor – sometimes even more than one. Someone who knows you well enough to understand you, but who is also detached enough to ensure the utmost objectivity of assessment and judgment.

In absence of a mentor, we must find one. As soon as possible.

But, above all, we must be willing to accept the feedback with an open mind, considering each piece of advice an opportunity for improvement, especially when it's hardest to listen to it.

Wherever there is a gap, tension, opportunity... there's a chance to grow. That's what we should look for. I would like to quote physics, which states that any difference in potential or pressure generates force. Let's make this very straightforward: electrical current flows because there is a difference between the electric potential of two single points. Wind blows when there's a difference in atmospheric pressure in two different areas, and so on.

In short, it's nature that tells us that force is generated when there is such a delta.

Force is generated when dreams exceed reality.

When the will is greater than the current result.

And when losing, that's when the team finds the energy to attack more.

That's how force is created.

Hence, there must be gaps. And that distance, which now disheartens you – for it reveals the gap between the current state and your potential, or between the obtained result and the hoped-for result – will be proportional to the force generated for your improvement.

It's nature. It's physics.

It's all defined by mathematical formulae.

That's why feedback, which highlights the gap between the current state and the potential one, is so powerful.

It is not by chance that Sheryl Sandberg, COO at Meta, claims that "feedback is the art of helping others see what they cannot see on their own". Author Frank A. Clark says "criticism, like rain, should be gentle enough to nourish a man's growth without destroying his roots".

A mentor is (s)he who can maximise the extent of all feedback, since they are close enough to comprehend the circumstances while also being objective enough to prevent emotions alone from setting the path.

Where there is feedback, there is a difference in potential. Hence, there is a force. There's a drive for growth and improvement.

That is true in sports, in any profession.

In life.

It's physics. It's mathematics.

"Success is the ability to go from failure to failure without losing your enthusiasm "

- Winston Churchill -

WHAT FAILURES CAN YOU RECALL? WHAT DID THEY TEACH YOU?

All athletes, at all levels, in any sport, have suffered great defeats. They have experienced bad days, bad races, matches gone wrong. They have lost in the very last minute, by a second or a centimetre. Recently, Roger Federer, one of the greatest tennis players in history, said he won roughly half the points he played. That's true, he won 54.1% of them. Djokovic – who ranks first in history in Men's Grand Slam victories – has won 54%, the same as Nadal. Serena Williams won 55%. These are some of the greatest and most successful players in the history of tennis.

What do these figures tell us? That they lose almost half of the points they play.

I would add that in a normal job, failing or losing half of the time would be quite a problem; it would be hard to get and keep a job with such percentages of success… From a mathematical standpoint, it means getting things wrong or doing worse than your direct opponent roughly half of the time.

Very complicated to handle.

Mathematically speaking, it would be extremely penalising. A sort of a sentence.

In sports, on the other hand, failure is part of the game. Do you remember Al Pacino? We quoted him earlier: "on any given Sunday you're gonna win or you're gonna lose. The point is, can you win or lose like a man?". Which for me breaks down like this: we must consider the effort shown on the pitch, the qualities fielded, and the teachings learnt from all circumstances.

What logic is learnt.

What motivation is reconstructed.

This is what happens on any given Sunday.

In basketball, it happens every three days.

And in tennis, it happens every day, or even twice a day. Several times a week.

Defeats, mistakes, disappointments… the difference between a player and a champion is the ability to convert these moments and these circumstances – which, by nature, are temporary – into lessons and motivations for the future.

Failure is an element of the journey.

It teaches resilience.

It puts humility to the test.

And it reminds us that success is never guaranteed.

For anyone.

Truth be told, defeats are also a driver for the future. The most painful defeats are the ones that set ablaze our souls and boost our determination, compelling us to work harder. To focus more on the details. To strive for excellence in every single skill or performance.

They either do that, or they turn off the light.

An athlete is defined according to their response to failure. As is the human inside the athlete.

It's that response that assigns the due value to mental and behavioural qualities.

That attitude makes that a human a real champion.

USAIN BOLT

In 2011 I had a false start in the 100 meters at the World Championships. I was injured that season, and I was not my usual confident self for such a big event. In the end, I learned that I had to always stay calm and trust my abilities. The race was won in a time that would have been comfortable for me. I learned from that, and it never happened again.

RONALDINHO

There is no way to measure failure. Any defeat or frustration caused by the expectations created can be considered a failure. The biggest lesson is to never give up and know that, if it's down to you, tomorrow will always be better than today or yesterday.

LANCE BRAUMAN

In my own small way, I fail every day, which makes this question a difficult one to answer. I see all failures as experiences to learn from. However much you hate to fail, what I have learned from each experience was probably more beneficial than anything else, and more motivating than the failure itself.

GRANT HOLLOWAY

I like to think that failures don't exist but instead only life lessons. You don't lose but you learn. From the races I've lost, I've always learnt something new about myself and from that experience.

WAYDE VEN NIEKERK

Certainly, my most recent injury. I think the biggest lesson learned was obviously how important it is to remain dedicated during your time as a professional athlete in which you have to make sure you remain focused and don't lose track of the current situation, your actual sport, your present objective. I missed out on a lot of opportunities and growth, and now I have to work even harder to get back stronger and to the level that I want to compete at.

XAVI

Perhaps it wasn't a failure as such, but I remember at the start of my career I was on the brink of leaving Barcelona, after the initial challenges that you face at the highest level and in a difficult club like this one.

However, in the end, and thanks above all to my mother, I decided to stay and fight for my dream. The final lesson is that you should never give up at the first hurdle, work hard and never stop believing in yourself. The route to success is very tough and you will always have to overcome difficult moments. The key is believing in yourself and working harder than ever.

KAKÁ

I don't like to talk about failure, because it's too strong a word to describe something in which you have given your best, but you've still not been able to succeed. But the defeats at the 2006 and 2010 World Cup, and the Champions League final with Liverpool, were all moments that showed me that any drop in concentration or distraction can spell the end of a journey that may have ended with victory.

TIGIST ASSEFA

I remember the 2016 Rio Olympics as one of my biggest setbacks. What I learned from that experience is the importance of working hard and never giving up.

STAN SMITH

I had four objectives. One of those was to be on the USA Davis Cup team. The second was to be the number one ranked player in the USA. The third was to win Wimbledon. The fourth was to be ranked number one in the world. The last two were almost level and the same, seeing the importance of Wimbledon. But I lost the Wimbledon final after leading two sets to one and truly believing I would win that match. That was a huge disappointment in 1971. Then in 1972 I was again in the final and I won in five sets, and it could have been the effect of the defeat the year prior, and so I definitely learned a lot from that loss.

CLAUDIO BERARDELLI

Sporting failure is perhaps the one thing I still struggle to handle emotionally. Defeat stays with me much longer and hits harder than victory ever does. But of course, without failure, we would never evolve. I named my club "2 Running Club" because, provocatively, I want the boys and girls I work with to remember that you can be a champion even when you're not number one. Probably my biggest failure — one I wrestle with every day — is managing my ego.

FELIPE SCOLARI

The Euro 2004 final with Portugal, played in Lisbon, with all our fans behind us, but we lost to Greece. Then the 2014 World Cup semi-final with Brazil against Germany, because of the big scoreline. There is no favourite in a match between Brazil and Germany, but such a loss was a huge disappointment for everyone. The lesson in both situations is always that no one is invincible, regardless of a favourable moment.

JACKIE JOYNER-KERSEE

Failure is not a word I use often. At the summer Olympics in 1984, I underestimated the power of mental strength while I was dealing with a knee tendon injury. I can honestly say my biggest disappointment in 1984 was my mental strength and support, which then always became increasingly more important.

ROBERTO MANCINI

I think that in football there are more failures than victories. When you play or coach for 20 years, you can't always win. It's the opposite and most times you don't win. But you always seek to improve on the things that didn't go well, and become meticulous, by looking back at what worked and didn't work. Sport is made up of wins and defeats, and when you get to a certain level, you can win or even lose a final: this is the price of always being at the top level.

ARRIGO SACCHI

The toughest moment was the time with the national team. Not only regarding how the World Cup went, but also all the difficulties that were created. Injuries, red cards, the weather conditions were brutal with forty degrees and one hundred percent humidity. We gave it our all, coming so close to winning despite everything seeming to be against us. Those players were heroes.

SERGIO GARCIA FERNÀNDEZ

I would not call them failures as such because they are the moments which in reality you learn the most.

An athlete's intimate, personal and mental relationship with their own failure accounts for a significant portion of their potential. It defines their humbleness, their ability to learn and improve themselves and handle pressure, as well as their will to accept circumstances, regardless of what they may be.

It puts to the test their determination and confidence.

And this doesn't just go for athletes, but for any professional who has set some goals and aims to achieve them.

This relationship between humbleness and confidence has always greatly interested me. It is often said that humble people lack confidence, and that confident people cannot be humble.

I believe the opposite is true.

I believe that a high level of confidence in one's own ability leads to a high level of humbleness. Because those who are very confident need not prove anything. You may have a huge ego, but self-confidence makes you aware that you don't necessarily have to prove anything. Actually, it always makes you test yourself, to constantly improve, which means acknowledging that there is still a lot of work to be done to bridge some gaps or to further enhance your strong points.

Presumption or arrogance are very different from confidence and are not to be mistaken for the relationship between confidence and humbleness. For example, putting yourself to the test is something you do if you are curious, if you test your limits, if you're humble enough to try and push those limits further up, thereby acknowledging there are shortcomings and room for improvement.

It's easy to say that failure is part of the journey, not the end of it. The problem is that all of this is comprehensible only when an entire life or career are observed from a wider viewpoint. How can we tell that to a footballer, when they miss a crucial penalty, in that specific moment or at the end of the match? Or to a tennis player who has just lost their first Grand Slam final? Without a broader context and a comprehensive perspective, failure is always and inevitably painful, disappointing, sad.

There is no immediate solution to that.

You cannot zoom out, as you do with a navigator, to picture that each segment is like a single step of a far longer journey, finding out that detours are sometimes necessary – or even beneficial.

Mathematics would tell us something quite simple. It's a time-related concept.

We only experience the moment, and we plan future moments.

No matter how painful a failure might be, it belongs to the past. There's no retrieving it, no mending it.

Physically speaking, that is.

From a philosophical point of view, on the other hand, feeling its burden is inevitable.

Either way, there are no alternatives. You must accept the facts, make the most of what they teach you, recall their meaning, and carry on with the journey.

In tennis, every single point is the most important thing in the world, when it is being played. As soon as the point is won or lost, it is in the past.

It's gone.

What matters now is just the following point.

The next point.

That will make all the difference.

The next ball.

The next game.

The next match.

There's always a next ball to be kicked.

"Practice as if you've never won.
Play as if you've never lost"

- M. Jordan -

NATURAL TALENT OR HARD WORK?

We have touched upon some reflections about talent in some earlier paragraphs. It represents the necessary foundations for the fulfilment of any dream. Under certain conditions. It's like better soil, which – given the same amount of sowing – can make a difference in terms of crop quality. Vice-versa, if the soil is the same, it will be the sowing and how the soil is taken care of that can offer a better yield.

Some time ago I was having lunch with Roberto Mancini; we were recalling the iconic characters of his time at Bologna FC, from the warehouseman to the youth team coach. What a magnificent period. Fragments of a long-gone football. Bologna is the city where I was born and raised; when I was a kid, everyone admired two young footballers, of the same age, who at 16 years old made their debut in Serie A (Italian top tier division): Roberto Mancini, from Jesi, in the Marches, and Marco Macina, from San Marino. In the 1981-82 campaign they were both in the first team of Bologna FC. We were 8 years old, and they were our undisputed idols.

Our heroes.

For some, including myself, they were absolute points of reference. For example, when I would practice taking free kicks in my room, with a sponge football. The bed was the wall, and I used to aim for the top corner, right beneath the desk. Truth be told, I also practiced celebrating. My personal goal celebration, the one nobody actually ever saw… a celebration that never made it to a TV show theme clip. Clearly, there was a lack of talent. Yes, that's more or less it…

The experts had no doubt as to who was the wonder boy, the most talented. Simply the best. He had a Messi-like potential, to the point that his biography is called "Era il più forte di tutti" (He was the best of them all).

Because it was true.

Based on sheer talent, Macina was number 1.

Mathematical.

His career never quite took off, for a number of reasons, and ended very soon, because of an ACL injury that entailed several complications. He played only 13 games in Serie A.

Roberto Mancini too was an extraordinary talent, but perhaps considered to be less outstanding than Macina. However, he became one of the best attacking midfielders in the history of Italian football: over 500 games in Serie A, scoring 156 goals; 62 caps with the national team (including both first team and Under 21), scoring 13 goals. Furthermore, he is also one of the most successful football managers in Italy and abroad (3 Serie A leagues, 4 Italian Cups, 2 Italian Super Cups, 1 FA Cup, 1 Premier League, 1 Community Shield, 1 Turkish Cup). He won in every team he played and with every team he coached, both at club and national level.

Two very similar talents, one of whom was considered to be better, but two very different stories, with a massive gap in terms of football honours.

It would be easy to simplify it all and play it down to mindset or ability to handle one's own talent. But reality tells us that there are a whole lot of stories like those of Marco and Roberto, a whole lot of athletes who are less talented than others, but capable of reaching fantastic goals, thanks to their perseverance, determination, discipline, tenacity and hard work. Those factors are also precious talents, it's not just about the technical skills. It's pretty much the same in the professional environment, it's not just about pure academic knowledge or subject matter expertise, the real difference is made of other attitudinal factors. The first being leadership.

Roberto was gifted with pure football talent, and he paired it with great determination, will power, and the ability to continuously improve himself. Plus, given his personal story, he was willing to make many sacrifices even at a young age, leaving his family and giving all he had to accomplish his feat. To complete his mission. With no guarantee of success.

Sometimes we hear the phrase: "what a waste of talent". True enough. It's a crime when talent is wasted because of a lack of will power. That very talent, which many don't have, and few are gifted with it, should always be respectfully upheld.

This concept isn't applicable to great sporting feats only. We all have some talent in a given field, or in some specific kind of behaviour, attitude, capability, or in some preference, subject or interest. The question is the following: are we doing justice to that talent on a daily basis? Are we nourishing it and practicing it as it deserves, through the work required for it to best express itself?

USAIN BOLT
It's a combination. You need talent to be a professional athlete, but I don't know anyone who reached the top without hard work

ALESSANDRO DEL PIERO
In my experience, it's a mixture of both. Natural talent gives you an advantage, but hard work is vital to hone your skills and have success.

RONALDINHO
Hard work complements natural talent. One cannot survive without the other.

PERES JEPCHIRCHIR
It's natural talent but also hard work. If you have talent but don't work hard you won't have success.

LANCE BRAUMAN

It's a bit cliché, but I would have to say both. In my experience finding the most talented athletes and convincing them that hard work maximizes their talent is still essential. Those are the athletes that experience success at the highest level.

NOAH LYLES

I think you need a high level of both. I think you can definitely have talent, and your talent can certainly take you very far. I've seen it in my life. But to break barriers and reach the top, you need to be able to push yourself to the limit, up until a level that will test you and will help you reach levels where talent alone is not enough. I firmly believe that a big part of it has to also be hard work.

GRANT HOLLOWAY

Both things. You need ability, which is a natural gift.

NATALIA GUITLER

It started with talent and then became hard work. I don't think any athlete, regardless of how talented they are, can establish themselves without a lot of hard work behind them.

XAVI

For me, it's a combination of both, but if I had to choose, I would say that hard work is more important than talent. Obviously, without talent, you can't win or reach the elite level, but the history of football is full of players with immense talent that did not have success because they didn't put in the work required at this level. In contrast, there are lots of examples of players with less talent that had amazing careers by making the most of their strengths through hard work and self-belief.

KAKÁ

It's a balance between the two, but you can obtain success without an enormous natural talent. Oppositely even if you have natural talent, if you don't work hard, you won't ever reach the very top.

TIGIST ASSEFA

Natural talent without hard work is nothing. Talent is important, but without consistent effort and discipline, it won't take you far.

STAN SMITH

You need a really big quantity of talent to be the best, to be a Federer, Djokovic or Nadal or one of the best players from down through the years. But the key truly is the hard work you put in and the commitment to getting the most out of your potential. And I really respect the ones that make the most of their potential rather than the ones who are extremely talented but don't work as hard.

CLAUDIO BERARDELLI

At the highest level, natural talent might give you the satisfaction of a few moments of success. But without hard and consistent work, you can forget about having a long career or evolving as much as possible as an athlete and as a person.

FELIPE SCOLARI

You need to do a lot of work. Dedication, study, you can have some traits to be a leader, which is natural, but dedication, observing and discipline are fundamental.

IAN THORPE

It's not just talent or just hard work, in reality it's a mixture of the two, as there are athletes that have the most natural talent but don't work hard enough to reach the levels they could, and there are athletes that work harder than anyone else, but seeing as they don't have natural talent, they won't ever reach the highest levels in sport. You definitely need a combination of the two.

JACKIE JOYNER-KERSEE

A mix of both. Talent needs to be nurtured. Natural talent gives you the foundations, but hard work is the main ingredient.

ROBERTO MANCINI

If someone has talent and also works hard, then they can go on to be a world class athlete. There are those that think talent alone is enough, and I thought this at the start when I was young. When you work seriously, listen to those who have more experience than you, coaches, teachers, then this is what makes the difference. Of course, talent is a real gift which cannot be wasted. You have to make the most of it by working hard.

ARRIGO SACCHI

Talent is something that you use to help the team. Then, hard work is crucial in making that talent effective during the game. A driver in F1 can't go 70 km/h all week and then hope to drive at 300 km/h on Sunday. He would crash. I've always believed in an attacking brand of football, controlling, creating the numerical advantage. This requires a lot of team spirit, beyond talent, and lots of hard work.

SERGIO GARCIA FERNÀNDEZ

It's a combination of the two. The perfect mix is talent, nurtured with hard work of continuous improvement.

COREY SEAGER

I think it's a mixture of both. But, in the end, I think hard work triumphs over talent. My father would always tell us that hard work beats talent when talent doesn't work hard. I've lived by learning from that principle for the entirety of my career.

The natural gift of talent is very precious, and we have the duty to protect it, nurture it and maximise it as much as we can. But talent becomes excellence only when it is tweaked through constant, consistent and persistent work.

In the initial phase of any career, the natural gift of talent – of any kind, be it technical, physical, intellectual – will always provide an initial edge, potentially significant, that enables you to shine in the short term.

But if we look at an entire career, in the long run, whether it's in sports or another profession, the maximum fulfilment of talent and its success-oriented equation can only occur through hard work, paired with great passion, dedication, determination and resilience. These are critical factors in all formulae for a long-lasting and replicable success.

Albert Einstein used to say that "genius is 1% talent and 99% hard work". A quote that perhaps stems from his great humbleness, given that his IQ (about 160) places him above 99.9968% of the population. But it is undeniable that the combination of talent and hard work is an absolute must, according to many successful champions. And, out of the two, it is hard work (even in the presence of less talent) that offers greater possibilities of success compared to greater talent paired with insufficient work – especially in the long term.

So, whether you like it or not, tenacity, sweat and constant improvement have been, are and will always be the discerning factor on the journey towards excellence, success and the entire fulfilment of one's own potential.

And that's great news, for it means that everyone – in different ways and in terms of talent put to use in very diverse areas – is given the opportunity to make it, somehow. To fulfil their potential through a more or less relevant amount of effort.

In the field of work, this concept is hard to discuss and to accept. Because everyone believes they are always committing themselves to the max. They believe that they're working extremely hard, more than anyone else, that they're the best and, sometimes, that their knowledge of the subject is more than sufficient. And, above all, nobody likes to be judged based on their hours of work, and rightly so. Therefore, only one assessment can be made and that is based on the hard results, which still depend on commitment, as well as capabilities.

Once the goal has been established, we ask ourselves: how much must I work to achieve it?

Students come across this sort of problem at school, when they prepare for a test, an exam or any kind of trial. There is never a moment when you can say "it's gonna be ok", simply because there is no limit to knowledge of the subject. There is no moment when we can say "I have studied enough", because we cannot even know how the memory is going to fare at the exam. So, what about repeating or writing one more time, over and over again. Theoretically, it's a never-ending process. Practice comes next and the line is drawn, meaning that, at a certain stage, we will arbitrarily (or compelled by a lack of time) conclude that we have studied enough to reach our goal. And we sit the exam. The same goes for athletes, for any race or match.

Bottom line: only the result matters. It's the only piece of information that tells us whether you have studied enough to reach your objective.

For sure, if the subject is difficult or if you are not geared for that specific sector, then you must prepare more. The contrary would not make sense in any logical approach.

So, going back to professional context, assuming sufficiency of the knowledge of the subject, then the analysis of the circumstances of the information, and of the options, are all crucial factors to the end result – the question is: how much is enough?

How much is enough to win the match?

This also goes for a lawyer who must face a prosecutor or a judge in court, for a manager who must deal with the company's competitors, or for a doctor or vet who must handle a medical emergency… when am I prepared enough?

The answer is never.

There is no mathematical certainty. It is the contingencies of time and life that make us draw a line and think it is what it is, and it will end as it should.

But the work required to attain excellence does not envisage a proper limit, and exercising a lot implies huge tangible benefits, especially at first. Then, over time, as abilities are enhanced, greater preparation may start making only marginal improvements, just like repeating a presentation a second time is greatly beneficial in terms of memory consolidation, while repeating it for the eleventh time will not produce the same incremental benefit vs. the tenth time in comparison of the second vs. the first round.

When to stop is related to personal sensitivity. Everyone has their own fate in their hands when it comes to deciding that when.

I believe that we can all agree that, if two athletes start on a par in terms of talent, it is commitment and the hard work to improve continuously, that make the whole difference, over time. Then, at a certain point in time, abilities reach their limit, at career end, when the maximum potential is reached. The complete fulfilment of one's potential depends on two factors: initial talent and something we can call work.

So, during the first year of your career, performance = initial talent.

These are the kids who dribble past all their opponents, they do tricks that was never taught to them and they're also the best when you field them with the older guys. Nobody knows why and then, all of a sudden, parents turn into coaches and/or agents and/or national team managers.

Or the child in primary school who is just given some basic information and then gets all of his times tables and additions right.

Over time, talent must be nourished with commitment, training, exercise. This generates a new value, the greatest one: current talent, which is constantly on the rise. At the onset, it grows more rapidly, then gradually slows down in time.

In a nutshell: performance = initial talent + (current talent*work).

TALENT + WORK EFFORTS IN 15 YEARS OF CAREER

— Talent rating 9

— Talent rating 9 minus 50% work

If you start with less initial talent, lots of hard work can bridge the gap with someone who has a greater initial talent that is never fully exploited through commitment.

So, as some champions say, sufficient talent paired with a great deal of hard work can exceed, in terms of performance, an extraordinary talent that is not fostered over time.

Nothing happens out of nothing.

There are no limits to constantly learning and improving.

This time, a click won't be enough to win.

*"A winning mentality is not something to apply once,
or when needed.
It's a consistent and persistent attitude
in living everything in every moment.
It defines who you are and motivates you
to overcome any previous limit, everything you do".*

WHAT IS A WINNING MENTALITY? ARE THERE SOME SPECIFIC QUALITIES THAT ARE COMMON TO GREAT CHAMPIONS?

There has been, and still is, a lot of talk about having a winning mentality in sports. That's understandable, given that, in sports, winning is not just one of the many options. It is rather an intrinsic need of sport itself.

I can't think of any sport that does not envisage a scoring mechanism to classify, evaluate or compare team or individual performances. That goes for both direct match races or games, and for seasonal rankings.

That might seem to conflict with the concept expressed by Pierre De Coubertin, the father of the modern Olympics and co-founder of the Olympic Committee: "The most important thing in the Olympics is not winning but taking part". A very powerful statement that carries great ethic, philosophical and educational value. Indeed, De Coubertin was among the first to offer a new value to sports and institutionalise a broader and idealistic point of view: its educational role goes beyond the result, it's a means to promote personal enhancement, self-discipline, honesty, respect, loyalty. In terms of winning, its philosophy was somewhat complex and surely rooted in human and cultural values, transcending the mere concept of outperforming an opponent. On the contrary, the goal was to compete with honour, respect the rules and opponents, better yourself and help create a more peaceful and harmonious world.

This complexity cannot be watered down to a simple statement: 'participating is what matters', for that would be a simplistic, wrong and deceitful interpretation. Sure, taking part in the Olympics is per se a great achievement, for all athletes. Being an Olympic athlete is a victory itself, something that will last forever. To the point that many Olympic athletes get themselves a tattoo of the five Olympic rings, marking their bodies forever – and, boy, would I have wanted to!

But in order to take part in the Olympics themselves, every athlete must qualify by winning the championships (or making it to a very limited group) of their own country. To represent your flag, you must be part of this very elite group. A group of winners.

Therefore, when it comes to an extraordinary event such as the Olympics – and all other world or regional contests – participating is following winning... not the contrary!

Ironically enough, you must win, a lot, if you want to take part!

Hence, winning matters.

It matters mathematically.

And philosophically.

Regardless of the kind of victory, whether it's defeating an opponent or beating your previous score. If there's a sport involved, there will always be a score, a time, a distance.

The Olympic motto is Citius, Altius, Fortius (faster, higher, stronger) ... the definition of exceeding a limit or beating an opponent. There is always an -er, which is the very fabric of sport, the philosophy of constant improvement, of beating previous limits and – yes – beating an opponent. Perhaps by just a few centimetres, just at the finish line... that will suffice.

Hence, you must do better, do more and win... and it's not just an option.

It works like that even at the amateur level. Take football for example: we train under the scorching sun, under the pouring rain and when it snows, we skip dinners, we rethink our personal lives, we make a lot of sacrifices... just to play with our team on any given Sunday. And win. Because it hurts when you lose. It does. And rightly so. If a defeat doesn't eat away at you, how can you even think you'll be competitive over a ninety-minute game?

I like to think that a winning mentality is not a momentary approach but a constant attitude, which imbues all aspects of living and thinking.

It's a way of feeling, interpreting and experiencing things.

A continuous and unwavering conviction that success is not just one of the options, but the only destination, and that it does not necessarily mean getting to the highest step of the podium. Above all, it means a constant commitment in overcoming all hurdles, despite adversities, with a confident and positive mindset, knowing that every challenge, every failure, every defeat is a new and extraordinary opportunity for growth.

It's always about putting in the utmost effort.

Utmost.

Effort.

Always.

It's about the force that urges us to give all we've got, and more, always, even and especially when nobody is looking. Constantly searching for excellence and courage and firmly believing that our dreams are at hand, if we're willing to work hard to fulfil them.

The force of a winning mentality is not just a tool for achieving immediate success. It should be considered a life philosophy, which drives us to constantly improve, to become more resilient, to have a steadfast faith in ourselves and our goals.

Having a winning mentality means firmly believing that, if you put in your greatest effort and never give up, no matter how difficult it may seem, you can reach any goal.

Carles Puyol, who spent his whole career at Barcelona, is, quite rightly, considered to be one of the greatest football defenders and captains of all time, owing to his skills, leadership and results. He taught us a very valuable lesson: "When I had the trials for Barça, my father told me, 'If you come back and they didn't pick you because there were twenty players better than you, no problem. If they don't pick you because there were twenty players who tried harder than you, don't bother coming home".

Utmost.

Effort.

Always.

USAIN BOLT

A winning mentality is being able to win when it matters. I was an athlete that performed better on the biggest stage. The bigger the prize, the more I thrived. I loved the energy of a packed stadium with the whole world watching. And, as I've said, the common traits found in great champions are talent, hard work, and discipline. I could also add motivation. I really admire the athletes who are still at the top level after many years. You need a lot of motivation to keep on going when you have already won everything.

ALESSANDRO DEL PIERO

A winning mentality implies resilience, a positive attitude, the ability to overcome challenges and a constant striving to reach objectives despite all the obstacles.

RONALDINHO

Having the conviction that every day, you can do even better. Successful athletes know they are role models for society, and I think it's important for them to do their jobs with joy, respect, and dedication.

PERES JEPCHIRCHIR

I think a winning mentality is not being afraid to lose or fail and always dream big. I am aggressive in what I do. Taking it all on with determination is fundamental.

LANCE BRAUMAN

Being able to find value in every opportunity, even when the objective is small or almost unattainable. The most successful athletes are guided by a large amount of inner strength. Their success is down to their love for the sport and their passion to win and have success, not for the money or fame which comes with it.

NOAH LYLES

A winning mentality is when you constantly learn. And for this reason, you will always be able to know how to put yourself in a winning position. And continuing to grow will ensure you will never lose.

GRANT HOLLOWAY

A winning mentality is the conviction to win at all costs, to reach the finish line first, and to be able to sacrifice what is needed to reach that result. We all want to win, whatever the circumstance or the probability.

WAYDE VAN NIEKERK

A winning mentality requires lots of calm and peace. If your heart is at peace and in the right place, your body will be calm, relaxed, and ready to perform at the highest level, which will push you to the highest level. I truly believe that if you invest in a balanced and holistic lifestyle, you will find your mental peace, physical and spiritual, and you will open the doors for your body to push itself to the limit and break barriers you have never done before. Successful athletes show great attitude, character and work ethic, and I've always tried to learn from them and use those lessons in my life.

NATALIA GUITLER

The awareness to say that you've done your job well, but at the same time, not allowing yourself to relax because you know your opponents will already be training hard to beat you next time. So, for me, it's the motivation to keep doing what I am doing and keep on doing it better so I can keep on improving and always be competitive.

XAVI

A winning mentality is not settling for what is satisfactory but always striving for excellence. Comparing it to school, if you study just enough to pass, it's normal to fail, but if you study aiming for full marks (10), you might not do it, but you will likely get a 9. If you train and aim for excellence or the best version of yourself, maybe one day you may not win, but you will come close, and you will learn from what you didn't do well so you can try to win the next time. For me, this is what having a winning mentality means: seeking excellence in every training session, in every game, or ultimately in life, in everything that you do. I think that all athletes with that winning gene never tire of winning and don't need external motivation to go seeking that next win, but they are animated by an immense inner strength.

SHAUNAE MILLER-UIBO

My objective has always been to be remembered as one of the best athletes in this sport. My mentality has always been to be the best, work harder and want it more than anyone else.

KAKÁ

It's the ability to take on challenges, work well under pressure, keep your integrity, and concentrate and dedicate totally to your challenge without ever losing sight of reality. The most successful athletes are focused on their goals, on when and where they want to arrive and on overcoming all the challenges that come their way. They maintain their determination to reach the highest levels that, when they started, they never imagined they would reach.

TIGIST ASSEFA

For me, a winning mindset means accomplishing the target I set for myself. Great champions share the attitude of staying focused, disciplined, and determined until they reach their goals

STAN SMITH

I think it's a combination of factors. It's your outlook on attitude and perseverance. You fight until the last point, and generally, the best players have a reputation for never giving up. Let's take the example of Federer or Djokovic; any of their opponents hope to have a close game since, for them, having a hard-fought game and losing can be considered a success. You want to develop a reputation as being tough, not only as a player but mentally tough, so if things go badly, you still remain difficult to beat. This becomes an advantage for everyone. The best player wins the match, and he is happy. The player who is not as good loses by a close scoreline but is happy, and so is everyone else. Look at a great player like Djokovic, and you can see he oozes confidence, always giving you the impression he can win even in difficult moments. The great players develop a reputation of never giving up, so it is hard to finish it off even if you are ahead. This belief can only be acquired after a huge amount of repeated practice. This is where we see the hard work at play to reach excellence.

CLAUDIO BERARDELLI

I believe the difference between great athletes and true champions lies more in their mindset than in their physical qualities. Even after more than twenty years in this world, I still haven't fully understood what makes champions so unique. I've been lucky enough to work with many great champions — often with very different personalities — but I've always had the impression that most of them shared a deep connection between their individuality and everything around them, without ever losing their sense of self.

FELIPE SCOLARI

Always believe you can win. Always believe you can go beyond your limits and break barriers. There is no win without being made to sweat for it. There is no success without dedication. Always believe in your own abilities and train with discipline, commitment and determination to overcome difficulties and reach your set objective. Everyone who has a winning mentality has a mixture of self-confidence, the desire to overcome obstacles and the drive to work hard to continuously improve with discipline, commitment, and determination.

IAN THORPE

A winning mentality is being able to arrive at any arena knowing that you have done everything possible to be ready for that moment. Great athletes have a few things in common, but I think it's the different character, mentality and attitude that allow us to have success. I don't think there is only one way or one type of athlete.

JACKIE JOYNER-KERSEE

A winning mentality is believing in yourself and being able to use every ounce of strength in your body to make it and reach your set goal. Athletes are united by this outlook and attitude.

ROBERTO MANCINI

A winning mentality is that of someone who wants to improve every day and who can't wait to train and improve. They think they can win any match or overcome any challenge, even when they don't necessarily have the qualities to beat their opponent. But in a match, anything can happen. That is the winning mentality. The thing that unites top athletes is always that. In all sports, the athletes with the biggest talent make enormous sacrifices from a young age: they leave their families and friends, and they don't get to enjoy their youth. It is the perseverance, determination and work ethic that pushes you to work even harder when things don't go your way.

ARRIGO SACCHI

A winning mentality emerges from the determination of a team, from its ability to work and to always strive for improvement. The things that the best have in common are putting the team first, working harder than their opponent, and continuously getting better.

SERGIO GARCIA FERNÀNDEZ

It's always believing in yourself. All successful athletes have a routine that they follow with discipline and consistency.

COREY SEAGER

Sacrifice and hard work. Winning is difficult and is not handed to you on a plate. You have to earn it. In baseball, every night, you have to make sure you earn it.

A winning mentality pools determination, resilience, positive attitude and a profound, staunch conviction in your potential, your abilities and your goals, regardless of the mistakes, obstacles or temporary failure.

It's not an action, nor a temporary attitude. It's a way of thinking and taking action.

It's a way of being.

A force that makes you give the very best of yourself, regardless of the circumstances.

Even, and especially, when nobody is watching, assessing or judging you.

It's the inspiration that motivates you to never give up before difficulties while viewing every experience as an opportunity for constant improvement.

As all champions say, the will, the need and the obsession for constant improvement is the hallmark of all successful champions.

There's never enough of it.

Every success is a new starting point.

Whether you're trying to excel in a sporting competition or reach your personal goals, this search for excellence calls for concentration, determination and courage.

I greatly appreciate what Ronnie Oldham once said when defining excellence. Something I often try to remind myself and the people I work with. A beautiful and simple phrase:

"Excellence is the result of caring more than others think is wise,

risking more than others think is safe,

dreaming more than others think is practical,

and expecting more than others think is possible."

A point of view that directs attention towards one's own goals, regardless of the rationale that may limit them.

Risk, beyond all calculations.

The dream, beyond all reality.

Expectations, beyond all statistical possibilities.

It's the denying of mathematics, science and statistics.

Because winning in sports and in life goes beyond all formulae, all expectations and all calculations.

It goes beyond self-awareness.

Just like the dream that transcends all rationality.

You cannot explain the dream.

When your skills don't quite make it… it's your heart that will.

When your talent doesn't get there … your willpower will.

When probabilities don't support your hopes… your courage will.

Thus, when qualities we might lack won't make it – such as skills and talent – and when there seems to be no chance of winning, it's up to our inner qualities, such as heart, willpower and courage, to step in.

I believe that there's one component of a winning mentality that is innate. It's to be found in the child who keeps on training, even when the time is up, or when their mother, from the kitchen, cries "Dinner's ready! Everyone take a seat!", until they net the damn ball in the top corner, or until all the target skittles in a tennis serve training session are knocked down.

You can see it in the coach who watches, over and over again, clips of the opposing team to prepare for the following match. How many must you watch? Who knows! As many as required. And how many are required? Who knows! But that coach will spend all night watching those clips, until he realises how to attack the opponents. That's when it's enough. And you know what? You can even avoid doing it… but someone will do it. When Carlo Ancelotti was working as an assistant coach to Arrigo Sacchi for the Italian national team, he would painstakingly go through the footage of the previous match, every time, and analyse the match statistics area by area. There were no algorithms, no software. He did it manually, fast-forwarding and rewinding a VHS tape.

The innate component of a winning mentality is also to be seen in a newly hired employee, when they are told not to worry because a given task is not urgent... and suddenly everything is done much sooner than expected, and even with that little extra thing, which was not a priority. Done straight away, earlier and better than expected. It's that co-worker you must never remind of all the details and that sometimes surprises you by showing you something that nobody asked for, nobody had wanted or thought of. But they did. Or that one who wants to know more, asks to do more, listens more, suggests more and expects more from himself than others expect from them.

Think of certain expectations for a specific job.

Some will do a decent job.

Some will do a great job, exceeding expectations, and you will never know how much and when they worked on it.

Some will do an extraordinary job. You won't be expecting it: it will hit you right in the face, out of the blue. It will exceed not only your expectations, but your imagination too.

All three of them might be out of the office the following second, to grab beers. One of them has handled the result, one of them has won, one has won and impressed.

The point is: how much do we expect of ourselves?

The good thing is that what really matters has occurred before, through a combination of talent, commitment and opportunity. So, it's what happens before our performance that will make the difference. How much are we willing to do, to give, to demand from ourselves?

And then perhaps we lose. Sure.

Losing is part of the picture. And, as we said before, defeat must eat away at you. Considerably. But just momentarily. We must then turn the page. Quickly.

We sometimes say, "don't take it personally". Really? Is there a defeat that is not personal?

"You couldn't do anything about it…" Seriously? So, who should have?

"This match isn't everything…" What do you mean, not everything?

Today, it is everything!

Right now, it is everything!

In that very moment, it must be everything!

Tomorrow is a new day, a different story.

We start all over again.

Today is everything. Tomorrow is nothing.

*"Winning once is a success.
Winning repeatedly is an attitude"*

- Unknown -

IS IT HARDER TO WIN THE FIRST TIME? THE SECOND? OR TO COME BACK AND WIN AGAIN?

Winning is not a logical, linear equation. After you've won for the first time, no linear path will lead you to the following performance. Sure, once a tennis player has won a Grand Slam tournament it is natural to think it is more likely for them to win another. If a sprinter has run the 100 metres in less than 9.9 seconds three or four times, it's logical to think they can do it again. It is plausible to think that they will have greater chances of winning compared to a sprinter who has never made it in less than 10 seconds. But it's not certain. It's not mathematical. Every sporting challenge is a whole other story.

By analogy, if you are particularly gifted in delivering presentations, it's very likely that your performance will be a consistently high-level one. But expectations may change, topics might create different complexities and questions can become thornier.

I would say the same goes for personal performance, in all professions: obtaining high-level results allows us to predict that said results can be replicated. But that will never be a certainty.

That's why we asked ourselves the question concerning the replicability of performance in sports, namely, how difficult it is to obtain the first victory compared to replicating that success later on.

John Wooden, a renowned American basketball coach, winner of 10 NCAA Championships in 12 years (National College Athletic Association, anyone living in the US is well aware of its importance, along with the NBA), and therefore knew something about success and the replicability of victory, once said: "Winning takes talent, to repeat takes character". It's a phrase that really struck me, because I get the impression it's almost natural to think you can win and make it the first time thanks to individual or team qualities, having no particular expectation. But after that, once you become a target, being the reigning champion, you are the athlete or the team to beat, hence expectations rise, and that calls for the development of a new mental strength for controlling and handling emotions. You must mature quickly, retaining the highest level of motivation while also coping with far greater pressure. After all, it's only the reigning champions who can lose their status.

Everyone else... has nothing to lose.

USAIN BOLT
It's harder to win a second or third time. I won my first Olympic title in Beijing in 2008. Following that, I set myself the goal of repeating the feat again in London in 2012. After that, I set myself the same goal again for Rio in 2016. This is something I am immensely proud of.

ALESSANDRO DEL PIERO
Each one presents a unique set of challenges. The first time is difficult because of a lack of experience, the second because of increased expectations, and getting back to winning ways is tough because it requires you to bounce back from previous failures or self-doubt.

RONALDINHO
Nothing is easy. Each stage of life and every day of work presents challenges that have to be overcome.

PERES JEPCHIRCHIR
It's harder to win the first time, because you've still got that fear of not being able to make it happen.

LANCE BRAUMAN

In my opinion and from my experience, it's harder to win again. An athlete at that stage has already reached the goal they originally set; so, having to dig deep to find that internal drive or that winning attitude to do it a second or third time, can be very difficult.

NOAH LYLES

I would say the second time. Winning again is the hardest task. The first time is the easiest because no one is putting pressure on you. No one is expecting anything from you. The second time on the other hand people have expectations. You also have your own personal expectations. And with these, doubts can creep in at times; you don't know if you will be able to repeat the trick. Winning again after a testing time is also very hard mentally because you might find yourself in a hole or mental space in which you have never found yourself before. You are below the line; you are behind from where you started on your first attempt. It's no easy feat getting out of that situation. You need to be incredibly strong mentally and have a lot of confidence in your abilities.

GRANT HOLLOWAY

Every time is difficult. The first is like opening a door while defending a title is difficult and can be extremely challenging. But what matters is turning up every day at your best and giving your all.

WAYDE VAN NIEKERK

I am currently in the comeback phase and so trying to get back to winning ways. It's certainly been one of the most demanding phases of my life and of my career. So, I would say winning again is extremely challenging, especially if you have achieved what is considered impossible in the 400 meters in track and field, to win again after an injury is very hard.

NATALIA GUITLER

In both cases, there are several obstacles. The first time is difficult because you know you've never done it before, and you are fighting for an objective that you've never reached. Doing it again is difficult, but you have the awareness of what is required and necessary to do it again.

SHAUNAE MILLER-UIBO

I think the most challenging aspect of any victory is continuing that path. The first one is always the easiest at that moment. You have nothing to lose but everything to gain. But after winning time and time again, it can be tricky to maintain that motivation or competitive spirit. This is why I think it's a good idea to set new goals after reaching a big one. It makes things exciting and enjoyable, and it makes winning again even sweeter.

XAVI

In my case as a footballer, I think the hardest part is winning for the first time, because with that comes the individual and collective confidence as well as the respect of others to win a second or third time. However, as a coach, I am also experiencing how difficult it is to get back to winning ways again after a difficult period, with a major sporting and economic crisis. It may seem cliché, but it's true: how easy it is to destroy but how hard it is to rebuild.

KAKÀ

It's just as hard or even harder to stay at the top than getting to the top. When you are at the highest level, you become the target for everyone, you are the centre of attention, you are the standard to reach and to beat.

TIGIST ASSEFA

The first victory is always the most difficult, because everything starts from zero. Once you achieve it, you gain confidence and experience that help you in the next one.

STAN SMITH

I think the first time is the hardest. Making the breakthrough, reaching unchartered territory. You don't know if you can do it until you make it happen.

CLAUDIO BERARDELLI

Without a doubt — the one that comes after failure.

FELIPE SCOLARI

When it comes to the game itself, you've never won until the game is over. You must play and compete for the whole time. There is nothing easy about it.

IAN THORPE

The first time that you win is definitely the easiest. I tell people that if you are a fan of the sport, you always cheer for the champions, if you are a fan of betting then you cheer for the underdog. The underdog has no pressure and can do anything without that expectation. When you are the champion, you have increased expectations, more pressure, more things you have to do to reach that performance while everyone else wants to beat you.

ROBERTO MANCINI

It's always difficult to win. Wherever. So, each victory is amazing. I think it's always harder to prove yourself again because a victory can also happen thanks to a slice of luck, but when you do it again and again then it shows you have the qualities to do it. However, every win is brilliant even those that may seem to be the easiest ones. You need to treasure each one with a lot of love.

ARRIGO SACCHI
I always started poorly because I always tried to immediately get the team playing in a certain way. Then when the methods and ideas are taken on board, and we started to hit form, we always did really well, until we became unstoppable. So, for me, each beginning was always harder. I remember after a 2 - 0 loss to Espanyol and Berlusconi asked me if I needed support and I said yes. He came to the training ground. He came by helicopter and instead of heading to the dressing room, he called everyone into his office. He could have made a really nice and clear speech, but on that occasion, he said only the following: "I have complete faith in Arrigo. Those who follow him will stay and will do really well, those that can't, leave. It lasted just 27 seconds.

SERGIO GARCIA FERNÀNDEZ
It's harder to win again, because even more doubts set in whether you have what it takes to do it again.

COREY SEAGER
I don't think one is ever easier than the other. Winning is always difficult and must be earned. No one will ever allow you to take something, no one will ever let you pass, and no one will ever give you an easy ride.

There is a certain convergence in considering the repeating (of a victory) harder than achieving a first victory, owing to the expectations and pressure mounting on someone who already has a successful track record, whose previous triumph is automatically considered a new starting point. This adds extra pressure on the physical performance and on the mental state, given the greater expectations. On the contrary, a first victory is always, by definition, that of an underdog, a challenger, who has very little to lose. If you're the champion, though, you are the only one who can lose the title, which is everything for you.

Expectations turn into a huge burden to be shouldered. Winning is great, but the more you win, the more it becomes the standard, unlike the first time, which was something extraordinary. Which is somewhat paradoxical, because, according to this rationale, while the first victory shall always be extraordinary, the following ones become ever more normal. And the pressure generated by the rising expectations is a burden that not all athletes can bear, for it implies an important mental task, which adds to all that is to be expected of an athlete's preparation.

In the case of the Olympics, where a gold medal is seldom defended, the fear of losing becomes a relevant element in the psychological handling of contests.

It is therefore a widely held opinion that defending the title is more difficult, and indeed a rarity, because it entails the ability to retain or improve one's competitiveness while also facing several psychological, motivational and tactical challenges that didn't exist when the first victory was obtained.

The same happens in many professions, to the point that failure makes more news than a repeated success, for the latter is taken for granted, as if it were standard. A financially solid and growing company makes the headlines when it is slowing down or bleeding red ink. Top executives who have witnessed five or six years of constant financial growth are fired after six months of mediocre results. That's how it works. It's a matter of expectations.

Winning can happen.

Winning again must be made to happen.

It sounds similar, but it's a whole different story.

Interestingly, as Peres said, we can never know that we're going to make it until we win, at least once. This is extremely relevant in a discipline such as the marathon. But it also goes for club coaches. In fact, some will never win. Others win constantly. It's rare for a coach to win just once.

In the professional sphere, making it the first time is always very tough. The first great presentation, the first high-level meeting, the first time you try to complete a complicated project. In that case, repeating oneself is facilitated by professional experience, which, alongside talent and commitment, is quite directly linked to the result. The twentieth plenary presentation surely has less of an emotional impact compared to the first, just as the second assignment is perhaps easier for the experienced professional who holds a similar responsibility already. The twentieth 200m race or the third Champions League final, on the other hand, might be a little less stressful, but their outcome remains a total mystery. It's always like the first time.

In order to replicate success, aside from attitude, it is also necessary to pay great attention to what has been learned in the positive path to the first victory. It is crucial to focus on constant improvement on that path to growth, but beware, for this might lead us to focus exclusively on what is wrong and must be changed. Instead, if we want to replicate our success, a critical portion of our attention must focus on everything that worked in achieving success the first time, which should be retained. It is key to start off again by understanding success, by retaining what has worked, so as to build an even greater triumph.

Someone said that "success inspires success".

We don't learn from our failures only, but also from our successes.

The moments and the circumstances may change, hence the variables. But the equation stands still, founded securely on our willpower and our mindset.

"Having a strong body is not sufficient. It's the mind that converts potential into results."

- Unknown -

ARE MORE IMPORTANT THE PHYSICAL OR MENTAL STRENGHTS?

Let's try to dissect an atom. Something that apparently cannot be split, being the result of gargantuan forces of attraction, which, by nature, cannot be separated.

Likewise, the mental and physical qualities of an athlete are highly symbiotic. So, did the chicken or egg come first? We basically want to understand the importance, correspondence and reciprocity of said forces, or qualities.

Resistance, muscular strength, speed, flexibility, coordination, power. The body.

Concentration, resilience, motivation, stress management, self-control, visualisation. The mind.

At first, these two dimensions or sets of forces might appear to be clearly separated. Stand-alone. Indeed, they can be trained and developed independently. But what if they affected one another? Just like, in Star Wars, the concentration of a Jedi could result in a supernatural physical strength so powerful that it could move objects or entire spaceships.

An athlete may be in top physical shape, but they might not be able to fully express their potential without the due mental preparation. Conversely, a mentally strong athlete might be able to offset some physical shortcomings, especially under great pressure. Synergy between these two aspects could be crucial for delivering a top performance, but which aspect comes first? Is one more important or decisive than the other?

What happens when a tennis player enjoys a huge comeback, in a match that was almost lost, saving two match points and then wins the match in the fifth set? It happens, but why? When does it happen? How does it happen? How much does the physique matter? How much does the mind matter? But, above all, which of the two features is easier to train in order to maximise your potential?

USAIN BOLT
Both are important. You can't be successful if you don't have both.

ALESSANDRO DEL PIERO
Both are key, but often, it's the mental qualities that get the best out of the physical qualities, especially when under pressure.

RONALDINHO
You can't excel physically if you don't have mental strength.

LANCE BRAUMAN
They go hand in hand. There's a reason why the best athletes are given the label "the complete package".

NOAH LYLES
The physical side is the easy part. The more you train, the more you strengthen your body. You can be the best athlete in the world, but if you're not mentally strong, as soon as you step onto that line, factors that go beyond the physical aspect will creep in, and you run the risk of losing because you won't have the strength, the confidence or the mindset necessary to win the race.

GRANT HOLLOWAY
When it comes to physical qualities, there is someone who will work harder than someone else, and I always want to be that someone who

works harder. The mental qualities help keep you consistent and coherent and give your all in the right moment.

WAYDE VAN NIEKERK

As an athlete, your physical qualities come naturally. So, it seems like child's play. However, when it comes to the mental aspect, things change continuously, and the mental effort required can sometimes exceed the physical effort. Therefore, I think that the mental aspect is the most demanding thing.

SHAUNAE MILLER-UIBO

I think both are just as important when it comes to being at the level of a professional athlete. You need a sort of physical talent, but it's key to be in excellent shape to manage the workload in training. Training is only one-half of it, and the mental side is the most important thing, especially when it comes to competing. For this reason, I have always said you have to enjoy yourself when you do it. You don't want to reach that limit, and your mind is elsewhere rather than giving your very best that day. When you have done all the hard work to the best of your abilities, then race day, at least for me, is the easiest part because the only thing left is the fun part which is competing.

XAVI

Mental qualities, without a doubt. Even in this case, without a minimum amount of physical qualities, you won't go anywhere, but look at me: I'm not very tall, I've never been fast or strong, but what has always given me an advantage has been being able to understand the game well, knowing where I need to be in that moment, where my teammates were before I received the ball, how to use the space or free up my teammates… and above all, the mental strength to compete at the elite level and deal with the pressure that comes with playing in front of

90,000 people or in a World Cup final. Mind over matter, without a doubt.

KAKÁ
Both are vital and have to be worked on in the same manner. Loads of sports, including football, focus more on the physical side and at times tend to forget, slightly, the mental aspect, but both things go together when it comes to success.

TIGIST ASSEFA
We cannot separate physical and mental qualities. Both are equally important, and you need them together to succeed.

STAN SMITH
It depends at which level we're talking about. At a really high level, all athletes are pretty talented and physically gifted, but the mental qualities make the difference and reveal the best players. Look at the three that have dominated the past 15 to 20 years (Federer, Nadal, Djokovic). They have extraordinary mental strength, not to mention their incredible inner drive to get the best out of their talent. Today, you cannot reach the top unless you are in really great shape; so, physical abilities are a given and a basic condition for everyone, while the mental side is the one that makes the difference. The part of talent, whether it be technique or mental, is not a given, but being physically at your best more or less is.

CLAUDIO BERARDELLI
The human being is such a complex system that trying to separate the two is, in my view, a huge mistake. It's probably the perfect harmony between these two dimensions that allows the best expression of one's potential.

FELIPE SCOLARI

In sport, you need both. The body has to be physically at its best, but without the competitive mentality, you won't go very far. The opposite applies: being mentally strong, but without the required physical preparation, you won't get to the end of the match or perform at your best performance possible.

IAN THORPE

When it comes to the physical and mental qualities at the elite level of sport, in reality, it varies in importance in different moments. Both need to be at their best at the same time, but you also need to be able to work with what you have been given. At times, you are working around an injury, so you need to compensate physically with another part of your body, and you need to be able to overcome this mentally in a way that you can be ready to give your best when the time comes.

ROBERTO MANCINI

The mental qualities are important because they are the ones that help you work more, be more committed, dig deep, and train better. If you are mentally weak, then you will struggle when the going gets tough. So, above all, you need the mental qualities, and then the physical ones can be improved a lot over time.

ARRIGO SACCHI

Mental. The mental approach is everything. It's what transforms a talent into a champion and what makes a player a great team player.

SERGIO GARCIA FERNÀNDEZ

Both go hand in hand. But if you have a lot of mental strength, then you have a huge advantage.

COREY SEAGER
I think both are equally as important. You need to be able to give a strong physical performance in the most important moments. But you also need to be able to deal with the moment and not let yourself be overwhelmed. It's vital to manage your own mental state to be able to get the most out of your physical talent.

    Both qualities, physical and mental, are decisive. No doubt about that. But what emerges from our champions' opinions is that mental qualities gain the upper hand.

    It is understandable that one must want to train, before actually training. In order to train properly, the proper will is necessary. In order to create a physical superiority (versus an opponent), superior mental intensity and commitment (versus an opponent) are required.

    Besides, it is also evident that physical qualities can be trained and developed by practicing, but only so much, depending on individual physical capabilities. The hardware is what it is, it also depends on genetics. It can be enhanced, but again, only so much.

    On the other hand, mental qualities are rooted in natural behaviour, habits and especially one's attitude towards things, work and life. They can be developed, theoretically with no limits to such development, because our mind's ability to adapt, improve and evolve is indeed unlimited. The software, the mind, can be updated, behaviour can change, attitudes can evolve.

    In sports, at certain levels, you must take for granted that the physical foundations are always there; hence the mental aspect often becomes the discerning factor for the overall performance.

While physical qualities are the visible foundations of success, the chassis of a car, the mental qualities are the engine and the invisible electronics. The body performs the action, but it's the mind that decides, perseveres and overcomes obstacles. Concentration makes you aware, resilience makes you get back on your feet every time you fall, motivation drives you to give your very best even when the body is tired. Courage and determination lead you to take that extra step, to lower your time by a tenth of a second.

Mental qualities transform physical qualities into tangible results. While physical preparation gives you the strength, speed and resistance required to compete, it is the mental qualities that determine when and how to put these resources to the best possible use.

When under great pressure – for example, in a final, or in a head-to-head race – the mind becomes the decisive factor.

It is concentration that allows you to perform the correct action at the right moment; it is resilience that makes you oust fatigue and difficulties; it is self-control that keeps you calm in a stressful situation.

The mind surely has some sort of predisposition, some sort of pre-tuned settings. But the good news is that it can be updated insofar as there is the will to do so. It's totally up to us.

We can decide whether we want to observe the others and their behaviour to better ourselves in sport, at work or in life. It's up to us.

We can decide to limit our responsiveness under certain circumstances, when we might say something, we could regret a fraction of a second after saying it.

We can decide to smile more often, to create a more serene environment, despite our concerns.

We can decide to dedicate our energies to a new purpose, mission or new challenge, if we believe we have completed our current path. Because there will always be more doors opening before us than the ones shutting behind us.

We can decide to take on a more positive approach in difficult times.

We can decide to avoid useless conflicts or battles.

Real strength is not to be found in muscles only, but in the mind's ability to convert every challenge into an opportunity for growth.

It is the mind that transforms talent into victory.

*"Gli atleti di successo non sono solo preparati fisicamente ma anche mentalmente.
I rituali sono strumenti di preparazione mentale che canalizzano l'energia fisica.
Un ponte tra il corpo e la mente."*

- Unknown –

DO YOU HAVE A RITUAL?
WHICH ONE, AND WHY?

Rituals are a series of actions, gestures or behaviours that are repeated regularly, following a specific order, often holding a symbolic or even practical meaning. Their purpose can be to give a sense of stability and concentration, possibly boding well for the future too.

Rafa Nadal, one of the greatest tennis players in history, used to follow some quite evident routines. Some actually considered them to be nervous tics. He did both of these routine acts before serving, when the player must reset all the feelings generated by the previous point, and when sitting down and resting between the odd numbered games. Describing those moments, he once said: "one sip from one bottle, one from another. Then I tidily arrange two bottles at my feet, to the left of the chair, one standing behind the other, diagonally facing the court. Some call it superstition, but it's not. If it were superstitious, why would I keep on doing the same thing even after I lose? It's just my way of entering into the match: tidying up what surrounds me helps me tidy up my mind".

Jannik Sinner bounces the ball five times before the first serve, and four times before the second.

I liked to play the piano every night before my university exams. It would relax me. I usually started off with Beethoven's Moonlight Sonata, an exercise for consolidating discipline and memory, followed by something I thought up myself. Always a different tune, an exercise of creative freedom, which allowed me to feel in my own way. The better I played it, the more I felt confident about my preparation ahead of the exam. If filled me with positive vibes.

In football, I would always tie up my shoelaces on the pitch, after the first few warmup kicks, because when I knelt down I could smell the grass, something that has always meant a lot to me and has always stirred up strong emotions (it still happens today, when I take just a few steps onto the pitch where my son – my striker! – is about to play).

It was a way to trace a temporal and spatial line: we would enter a timeframe dedicated to football, a space that outlined and represented it. That was my entire world for ninety plus minutes … everything else stayed outside. Still today, whatever sport I may practice, whether it's on a pitch, a tennis court, a tarmacked street for running, a ski slope… I still can't help tying or fastening my shoes or boots once I'm on that surface. And still today, as I wait for the day's first meeting, I will roll up the long sleeves of my t-shirt or sweatshirt to trace that line.

These are powerful rituals which, through their repetition and through the meaning we attach to them, can influence our behaviour, feelings and mindset.

They are comforting, reassuring, propitiatory, anyone can give them the meaning they prefer. Whether they are right or wrong, true or false, has no relevance whatsoever.

They work as switches of the mind and spirit. They transform the ordinary into extraordinary, preparing us to overcome every challenge.

Making us our own special heroes.

USAIN BOLT
No, I don't have any sort of ritual.

ALESSANDRO DEL PIERO
Yes, before matches, I had a ritual involving some mental preparation, thinking about what might happen and a specific warm-up routine to ensure the best performance possible.

RONALDINHO
No, I didn't have any rituals during my playing days.

PERES JEPCHIRCHIR
I'm a Christian and believe in God. I have no other rituals.

NOAH LYLES
To be honest, yes, and I think the only ritual I have is to visualize how the race will unfold. The other things, such as being prepared and hydrated, I wouldn't call rituals because it's a normal part of the preparation. I think a ritual is something someone does and that doesn't have any real significance. But you know, going back to the visualization, and if you don't do that, then I don't think you are truly ready to compete.

GRANT HOLLOWAY
No, no ritual, only hard work. I try to remain coherent and consistent; this is the most important thing for me.

NATALIA GUTLIER
Yes, my biggest ritual today is my warm-up ahead of a race, which is always the same. Then, when it comes to the race, I always kiss the red ribbon I wear on my arm, which symbolizes the protection and energy I'll be blessed with during the race.

SHAUNAE MILLER-UIBO
I don't really have a ritual as such, but I always talk with God during my warm-up. While I'm out on the track, just before starting my race, I'm happy to let myself go and totally surrender myself to Him. And I believe everything he has for me is for me. And it doesn't matter what the result is, in any case, I will always be grateful.

XAVI
No, not really.

KAKÁ
I don't have a ritual, because this is closely tied with an obsession. I am a man of faith, and I try to study, understand and follow what I believe in.

TIGIST ASSEFA
Yes, I am an Orthodox Tewahedo Christian, and I follow practices that reflect my faith in my daily life and before competitions.

STAN SMITH
Yes, a ritual that I hadn't even thought of before I became involved in coaching was my pre-serve routine. I would bounce the ball twice before the first serve. If I failed on my first serve, I would then only bounce the ball once, pause, and then serve again. My ritual would be to bounce the ball, stop, and visualize where I would hit the ball. Thinking about it, a funny thing happened. I was practicing with Bob Lutz, my doubles partner, and we were both warming up for a singles match. We would warm up together, and I was serving really well, and his return was even better. So, I shouted from the other side of the court: "Bob, my serve is fantastic but how can you return so well?" He said, "Well, you're looking where you're going to serve every single time, so I know where the ball is going." So, I said, "Well, Bob, how long have I been doing it?" He said: "About 10 years." I responded, "Thanks! Thanks for only letting me know now!" I also had a routine in my pre-match warm-up. I also had some superstitions, such as always going to the same locker when I went into the changing room unless they had already been assigned. I always chose the same locker, I used the same shower and things like that, which were a bit over the top.

CLAUDIO BERARDELLI
I'm not superstitious, but I always carry a stopwatch with me — even when I'm just watching a race on TV and don't really need it. Maybe it's my way of feeling like a coach — always and everywhere.

FELIPE SCOLARI
I say my prayers before a match; my faith has always been important to me.

ROBERTO MANCINI
Yes, I had rituals when I was younger, you know, the usual things such as always tying my shoelaces the same way, stepping onto the pitch with the same foot, or always doing the same things the night before a match. A load of silly things.

ARRIGO SACCHI
No. No ritual. But lots of my players had them.

SERGIO GARCIA FERNÀNDEZ
No.

When it comes to rituals, there is no consistency; there are no methods, structures or equations.
There is no logic, no rationale.
Some athletes have them, some don't.
Half of the sixteen champions we interviewed on this topic have a ritual, the other half don't. Some use them as a way for transiting into their concentration zone, others to fill their spirit.

I believe that rituals, despite their random and rather naïve nature, have a profound and positive effect on our spirt, for they create a connection, a meaning, a sense of inner safety.

Sure, they're just habits… simple habits. But they're also powerful tools that can help the athlete prepare to shine. They lay the mental foundations for a better performance; they connect mind and body, in harmony, ensuring access to an intense and intimate zone of wellbeing. All rituals revive a motivational drive that helps athletes overcome their fears, shine under pressure and make every challenge an opportunity to stand out.

But they are also a promise we make to ourselves. A creed whose aim is to help us overcome pressure. The real power of rituals is to be seen in their ability to convert uncertainty into clarity, fear into strength. They pave a clear path that goes from preparation to the moment of truth, channelling all energies in the critical instant.

They act as a switch that maximises concentration, as if to say: now or never.

*"Success is no accident.
It is hard work, perseverance, learning, studying, sacrifice
and most of all,
love of what you are doing or learning to do."*

- Pelé –

IF YOU HAD TO GIVE THREE PIECES OF ADVICE TO A YOUNG, TALENTED ATHLETE, WHAT WOULD THEY BE?

The new generations, unlike mine, were born in an on-demand world.

They can call or videocall the whole world, at any time. They can order a product in any shop, supplier or website, in any country, and receive it anywhere. Sometimes, it will only take a few hours.

They can see any type of created content anywhere on the planet, in real time. They can access, download and view any film, on any device, at any moment.

They can watch, stop or pause.

They are, quite simply, in control of everything.

I remember when I used to plan my afternoon: homework, football with my friends, then quickly back home, in front of the TV, to watch the latest episode of Captain Tsubasa.

It couldn't be paused.

It couldn't be stopped.

The anime wouldn't wait for us.

It was being aired then, in that specific moment. So, it was either then, or it would be gone.

Everything was a little more complicated: even the simplest thing required some sort of effort. Going shopping to buy a new pair of shoes, for example, perhaps meant having to go to five different shops because nobody had the right size of the Adidas World Cup shoes. We had to get organised to do everything. Today, shoes can be ordered online. All it takes is a click. Leaving the house is by no means necessary.

As for holidays, there were no low-cost flights. We would wander across Europe with a rucksack, hopping from one train to another.

There were no Ryanair or Easyjet flights. What we had was the Interrail, a sort of European continental second class season ticket. Lots of humanity, little planning, big hassle, and lots of sweat and patience.

Watching TV (everything was live, it couldn't be recorded, until around 1985), going to the cinema and hoping to find a seat, to avoid queuing up for nothing.

We were accustomed to these lesser victories, the conquests of the day. They were almost worthless, yet they gave us the feeling we had done something… to achieve something.

Without doing something, nothing would ever fall into our arms.

And that's pretty much the essence of sports, and of life.

I too found myself caught in a generational clash when my father reminded me that he went to school on a lorry carrying soldiers, which regularly transited through his neighbourhood at 5:30 am. That was during the war. And the way back? Twelve kilometres on foot. I, on the other hand, rode my moped to school. Before I turned 14, my big hassle was taking the bus, for only three stops…

I would not raise the issue of the soldiers' truck with my children, who already feel discomfort and sluggishness at the mere mention of the word 'truck,' and fortunately, they know very little about war.

But today's education, sacrificed for the sake of everything, always, now and on-demand, has deceitfully led to the belief that even the world is at our disposal. That doing something to obtain something is an obsolete and unfair concept. Everything is owed to us. Being promoted at work is owed (yes, but what about your results?), the performance is owed (yes, but what about your preparation?), and if I have worked a lot then I deserve a good mark (yes, but how many correct answers did you give?).

This has somewhat separated one's own will from one's individual performance compared to others.

Not only is everything owed to us. It is owed regardless of the competitive context. So, adding the competitive context to the previous questions: promotion is owed (yes, but what about the colleagues who are better and performed better than you?), performance is owed (yes, but what about your preparation, compared to that of your opponents?), if I have worked a lot then I deserve a good mark (yes, but how many correct answers did you give and how did that fare compared to your class mates?).

Here's the thing: the world, like sports, cannot be paused. Results are not on demand.

There is no privilege to be enjoyed before the finish line or the final whistle.

There is no merit before the result is achieved.

There are no pre-awarded medals.

There is no booking a victory with an app.

Nor can a promotion be ordered.

In sports, success is a constant balance between passion, commitment and preparation. Personal will and lifelong learning underpin all improvement, all progress, fuelled by that strong passion that drives athletes to give their very best, always. All athletes, all professionals. All husbands, wives, parents and friends.

Entertainment keeps enthusiasm alive, constant training consolidates basic skills and further hones them. Concentration and the desire for victory guide all actions, supported by confidence in ourselves and in the process.

Respecting ourselves, the opponents and the game is crucial, as is the ability to overcome obstacles and handle pressure in critical moments. Discipline and determination are the pillars underpinning mental preparation, while teamwork enhances individual efforts, converting them into a collective success. Believing in the process and in one's ability to grow and improve is the path to victory.

USAIN BOLT

I talk a lot to young athletes, and I always tell them to work hard, enjoy themselves and surround themselves with good people.

ALESSANDRA DEL PIERO

Focus on learning and continuously getting better. Lead a balanced life. Never lose sight of your love and your passion for sport.

RONALDINHO

Never forget where you came from. Live your life and work with a smile on your face. Your biggest reward will be the happiness of others.

PERES JEPCHIRCHIR

Be disciplined. Have patience. Believe in yourself. But you will need a lot of hard work.

LANCE BRAUMAN

Always do your best. Follow your path. Represent yourself, your family and your community by making the most of your abilities.

GRANT HOLLOWAY

Remain consistent on and off the track. Stay "coachable" and keep your feet on the ground. Surround yourself with a positive group of people.

NATALIA GUITLER

Choose carefully what you want to do and devote yourself entirely to it. After choosing, give all your energy, passion and life to make it happen. Never forget to have fun and to be happy with the path that you have chosen!

XAVI

Train every day as if it were the last and learn as much as possible from all your coaches. Never stop believing in yourself. Always show respect for your teammates and opponents.

KAKÁ

Make sure you have people around you who want the best for you and remind you of where you came from. Make sure you keep your feet on the ground. Always have an objective and devote yourself entirely to it, and don't be arrogant when you reach it; instead, set yourself a new goal and start again. Be ready for the pressure and seek out help when it becomes tough to deal with it. We all have fears, and we all feel insecure and nervous, but if dealt with in the right manner, it can help us succeed and move forward.

TIGIST ASSEFA

If I could suggest three things to a young talented athlete, they would be: love your work, work hard, and stay disciplined.

STAN SMITH

Establish, as soon as possible, good technical fundamentals. I've seen a lot of players in their careers constantly making changes to their game and pretty big changes, such as their grip and so on. Good fundamentals and good practice, with an aim. Train with total concentration and with a purpose, with every hit. Every time you hit the ball, you must be trying to do something; you could be trying to aim for a specific target near the baseline. You could be trying to hit it hard. You could be trying to hit it smoothly. You could be trying to mix up your shots but make the most of your time on the court. You are not only hitting those balls for four hours. Some players think that training four hours a day will make them great players. If you play four hours a day and hit the ball randomly, when it matters most, when you want to hit that ball down the sideline, two inches from the line, hit a passing shot or hit a serve to a specific part, you won't have any confidence to do so. But if you train with a goal and keep on doing so with success, you can do it. This is what will make that happen. This is the second thing. The third thing is to enjoy the process. The best example for me at this moment, at least from what I can see, is Alcaraz. He oozes joy for the game. And it seems that he likes the journey he is on and that he will do well. Obviously, he has incredible talent and a great coach, right from the start and now. He knows his weaknesses and his strengths and is working on his weaknesses and strengths. He is, therefore, really determined.

CLAUDIO BERARDELLI

Time is a fundamental ingredient in high-level sport. So patience is a trait that can truly make the difference.
Surround yourself with people who can really make a difference — few, but the right ones.
Remember that you are a special human being, given a rather rare gift — and perhaps that gift comes with a responsibility to accept.

FELIPE SCOLARI

Be disciplined. Have a lot of dedication, determination, and discipline. Be actively involved in the group and always be prepared physically and mentally. The career of a professional athlete is short. It lasts around 15 years. There is no time to lose.

IAN THORPE

Find out as early as possible what it is you love about your sport so that it becomes the most important part of what you do. For me, it was discovering the way I was able to move in the water in a different way to others. The next thing is to listen to your coach or your teachers, the people around you that help you 95 percent of the time; the other 5 percent, you should listen to yourself and what you think is best for you. The third thing is that it's a very difficult process, and when it becomes difficult, and it will become difficult, you need to keep on reminding yourself what you want to achieve and stay focused on what the long-term, medium and short-term goals are.

JACKIE JOYNER-KERSEE
Enjoy it. Work hard. Stay humble.

ROBERTO MANCINI
I think passion is vital. If you have passion, you are already well on the way. Then, be professional, determined, persevering, and confident because your time in sport won't last 40 or 50 years. Then, always be extra committed even when you think you have reached the top, because you can always go higher. I think that you can improve by working seriously day in and day out at any age.

ARRIGO SACCHI
Don't be arrogant and think you have made it. Don't be too assertive or think as a soloist or as an individual. Play with the team, for the team, across the pitch and for the entire time. This is what can make you a hero, which means giving everything that you have.

SERGIO GARCIA FERNÀNDEZ
Work hard. Believe in yourself. And the most important of the lot is to love what you do.

COREY SEAGER
Don't ever settle for second best. Never stop working hard. Be humble.

In sports, success is a complex journey that unites mind, body and spirit in the pursuit of constant growth. At the very centre there is an immeasurable passion, that inner flame which fuels the desire of continuously improving every single day. This love for sport motivates the athlete to constantly learn and continuously strive to improve all aspects and each dimension of their own game, from basic skills to the mental strategy.

Giving one's best is therefore not just an objective, rather it becomes a daily standard. Without a predefined limit to where the bar is set.

When commitment and entertainment blend together, maintaining a strong sense of enjoyment and fun, all challenges can be faced with a sense of enthusiasm and light-heartedness, and without losing sight of how important the disciplined training is. It is under such training that discipline and determination are developed – two key elements for constructing a complete athlete.

The road to success also requires great concentration and a deeply rooted will to win. However, success is not measured in terms of victory alone; it is also the ability to overcome hurdles, to adapt and grow amid difficulties. That's what defines a champion. Coping with pressure is an attitude that grows stronger as experience is gained, hence mental preparation becomes crucial for maintaining focus and calm in decisive moments.

Success also requires an unwavering faith in one's own potential and in the path undertaken, namely, believing in the process and in oneself. Should this conviction fall short, it's easy to lose sight of the end goals.

Furthermore, respect for ourselves, for our opponents, for our teammates and for the game is fundamental. Respect forges the environment where true greatness can emerge.

Finally, sport is never an individual endeavour. Teamwork and a sense of belonging to a group provide the collective energy needed to take on the greatest challenges. Synergy between individuals in a team enhances the effectiveness of everyone, thus making it possible to achieve goals that would otherwise be unattainable, individually.

In short, the formula for success in sports is a harmonious combination of passion, dedication, learning and growth, guided by a strong and determined mind, and when the mind is not enough, then a boundless willpower should extend the reach – beyond any reason.

"To be successful at anything,
the truth is you don't have to be special.
You just have to be what most people aren't:
consistent,
determined
and willing to work for it.

- Tom Brady –

THE FORMULA OF THE FORMULAS. CONCLUSIONS.

There are some words we just don't like. They can hurt our pride a little, or they can make us defensive. Because it's always easier to feel like we have already done everything possible and observe the problems and limitations that elude our control rather than trying some self-criticism.

It's called locus, or, more specifically, locus of control. I learnt it during an excellent training course I attended in the early years of my career, one of those courses that changes one's point of view forever.

Simply put, in psychology, the locus of control is the modality through which every individual views their life's events – both successes and failures – as a consequence of their behaviour or actions, hence internally controllable and dependent on one's ability, willpower and capacity. Or these events may be the result of single external causes that lie outside one's actions or willpower, such as luck, chance or fate.

Basically, locus is external whenever "it's not my fault, it's not up to me, I can't do anything about it, it's beyond my willpower or my actions, it just had to go that way". More commonly known as bad luck. On the other hand, locus is internal when we are convinced that there is always something we can do to take our fate in our own hands, to do something, to change or improve any circumstance, to find positive or productive solutions even when everything feels like it's going south.

Some studies link this locus to the level of self-esteem, for the latter is remarkably affected by our conviction of having control over our results and by the awareness that failure can be remedied effectively. But a locus of control that is excessively internal also leads us to constantly blame and criticise ourselves, which in turn steps up the pressure we must shoulder. Then again, it also increases tension as we aim to constantly improve.

Vice-versa, an excessively external locus leads us to shrug off responsibilities and results with lesser ambitions, low levels of commitment, greater vulnerability to stress and slow recovery following a failure. It can even increase the risk of developing anxiety and, in the most pathological cases, depression.

There is no overarching rule; it is rather a spectrum where everyone has a preferred and aptitude-related locus but, depending on the circumstances, the instinctive approach may vary, and the same individual might tend to follow a different locus, modifying their perception of things and the meaning they attach to them. Therefore, there are circumstances under which locating a problem externally is normal even for those who tend to have an internal locus. Being a teenager in 2020 is fortuitous, I'd say. There's nothing that can be done about that. But then it's up to the individual to find acceptable, constructive or even positive solutions, under dramatic circumstances.

For athletes, an internal locus of control is somewhat associated with the adoption of a more determined and proactive approach, which also brings greater psychological wellbeing, when heading towards a goal – though this goes for any kind of person or professional. It is to be found in those who take on challenges with great determination, always raising the bar of ambition, who have superior problem-solving skills and are able to better exploit their inner resources. Overall, it's about approaching challenges and life with an inborn need to do something in order to obtain something, knowing that it is always possible to act first-hand to guide one's life, to obtain a result which – bottom line – is up to us.

Concluding, the locus of control greatly affects a sportsperson's perception and assessment of their performance, as well everyone's assessment of their own life or job. Victories and defeats, for athletes, just like personal successes or failures for us, alternate continuously. It's inevitable. What matters is not so much the result, per se, but rather the perception of one's ability to influence present and future results and the propensity to take on direct responsibility for one's actions. Always learning, improving and delivering the maximum effort.

But what does the fulfilment of one's potential – in sports, in life, at work – truly depend on?

It's a choice.

We can choose. We may be convinced there is always something we can do to fulfil that potential, to make it real. That choice sparks a series of actions that define who we are, how we behave and what we're willing to do to reach fulfilment.

Going back to what our sports champions said, some specific concepts and key words emerge unmistakably.

Simple words, which call to mind real emotions.

At least for me.

I can count eleven of them. As many as the starting players in a football team.

1) Passion, beyond any reason.

Passion cannot be ordered. It cannot be commanded. It cannot be put in an Amazon cart, nor can it be added to the Netflix list of favourites.

But it can be felt. It can be perceived in that inner flame that urges us to make that little extra effort compared to what is standard. It's that strength that leads us to firmly believe in our abilities, especially in times of defeat.

It's that enthusiasm we feel when doing things, which doesn't stem from a rational logic or from a specific will. It's pure, childlike instinct, which just turns on. There's no controlling it.

Passion is the fire that sets dreams ablaze. It shapes them and makes them real. It converts them into tangible goals, to the point that, every morning, it wakes us up and conveys to us the enthusiasm for taking on a new day, working hard to achieve what we love. Passion is the engine that drives all athletes. Without passion, daily training sessions would just be tiring, and challenges would become insurmountable obstacles. In sports, passion is what turns mere interest into a real vocation. It's the enthusiasm that transforms long and difficult training hours into moments of joy and growth. It makes the difference between performing a task and feeling part of a mission.

When?

Always.

Because passion has no switch. Just like a mission has none. One lives for the mission, not the opposite.

How can we turn on that passion?

We can't. It just happens.

It overwhelms us.

Time flies, there's no stopping it.

What can I do if I have no passion for what I'm doing?

Perhaps you're doing the wrong thing. If you're asking yourself this question, and if the answer confirms that you're not doing what you love... well, your fate is in your hands. You can always try to change it.

Life is too short to do something we don't like.

A famous aphorism reads: Working hard for something we don't care about is called stress. Working hard for something we love is called passion.

Simple, prosaic.

But very true.

We have all experienced it.

The real question is: how to find our passion?

I believe there are two ways.

One is that of experimenting, trying, watching, observing and accepting the experiences that are offered to us. We decide to make little children try all sports rather than the sport we like, because not all passions are handed down genetically. It will be up to them to decide. Actually, it's their passion that will decide.

We should observe what children do. Those little obsessions for activities that consume them and their time, in which they get lost. And let's try to remember what used to absorb us when we were kids, or what still absorbs us now, drawing us to it like a black hole.

Observing, recalling and, not lastly, feeling what we felt when we did something. Not what our mind tells us or told us, but the feeling that bypassed all cerebral activities.

My brother used to build things. All sorts of things.

I didn't even know where to begin.

My sister used to study a lot: she was excellent at Italian, Greek and Latin. And she even liked that.

I was a zero.

Today, he is an engineer who builds racing engines, and she teaches Italian, Latin and Greek.

Surprise, surprise.

Then we must try to understand where we feel a disproportionate gap between improvement and commitment. Usually, we develop a passion for activities we instinctively like, or for activities in which we achieve disproportionate results with a reasonable effort. That's what triggers a new commitment, for trying more, which implies even greater improvements, yet more passion, which again fuels further commitment, and so on.

It's mathematics: it's the exponential function.

Because we like doing things well. It's human, we develop a passion for what we're good at.

And passion, real passion, can take us a very long way.

2) Desire to win. Beyond any calculations.

The desire to win exceeds all expectations: it is the inner force that pushes us beyond previous limits, making us achieve the unimaginable. It is a dark, primitive, instinctive force, and it's not just about conquering medals or silverware; it's about overcoming challenges, proving to ourselves that we can do a lot more, that we can fulfil our potential and attain what we, and others, thought was impossible. It's that energy that makes us think "I can do it" even when the tide has turned against us.

The desire to win can and must be trained.

It translates into that stubborn determination to hit all the six target cones placed in the serving area before packing up everything, turning off the floodlights and leaving the tennis court.

And what if we don't make it?

We continue.

It's that little obsession that makes us want to solve even the last equation before going to bed.

And if we don't solve it?

We persevere.

And if it really cannot be solved?

It doesn't matter. Sooner or later, it will be solved.

And when that happens… we will have won.

Because wanting to win is the very first victory.

3) Courage. Beyond any fears.

Winston Churchill once said: "Success is not final. Failure is not fatal. It is the courage to continue that counts"

Turning the page, always believing in it, persevering. When we're really keen on something, the fear of failing is countered by our inner courage: it drives us to tackle difficulties, overcome obstacles, take on risks and responsibilities.

Courage too can be trained.

Through trial and error.

Trying. Falling. Getting back up. Trying again.

Failing means having attempted to deliver any kind performance which, in that given moment, under the given circumstances, for some specific reason, was beyond our tangible reach. Sometimes, it's just a matter of time. Training to cope with failure is good for us, because courage is not the absence of fear: it's the ability to handle it, preventing it from negatively impacting today's result, so that a better result may be achieved tomorrow, having overcome the initial fears.

Being courageous every day is fundamental for all athletes. We must face the fear of failure, compete at the top levels and leave our comfort zone.

Without courage, even the most promising talents can freeze, incapable of exploring outside their familiar comfort zone.

4) Willpower, beyond any obstacles.

When we look away from our goal, we notice all the obstacles lying between us and it. They disturb us, they threaten us, they distract us. Willpower keeps us focused on the goal. It's what drives our stubborn perseverance. It's what keeps us on track even when we swerve, when the path becomes winding, when challenges seem insurmountable or when results are not there yet.

It's the will to get started. The will to try. The will to improve. The will to continue, or to change.

It's a choice.

Everything begins with a choice.

It's the human way of setting a specific path, regardless of the circumstances that may divert it.

It's the choice we make through willpower that characterises us, defines us, makes us invincible, regardless of the result.

And yet, let's speak plainly: how much do we desire ... the thing that we desire?

Because it doesn't come free of charge. Willpower represents what we're ready to invest, before any direct return.

What are we willing to give for sure, to obtain what we really want, without any certainty?

5) Sacrifice, beyond any immediate rewards.

Once the choice has been made, through willpower, success becomes a consequence of hard work and sacrifice. We must sow before we reap. We must give before receiving.

It's a sort of blind bet; it's an unescapable stage on the path to excellence. It's a toll that must be paid. Not everything will be easy and comfy, sometimes something must be given up when pursuing a goal.

Plus, there is no guarantee that our sacrifices will be repaid proportionally. It's a non-refundable investment.

Athletes often must give up time with family and friends, daily pleasures, other activities that are not compatible with their goals.

Sacrifice is the price to be paid to reach extraordinary levels, and acknowledging it is crucial to retain motivation.

Who's forcing us to do it? Nobody.

Sure, everyone says that their sacrifices have been repaid. We're talking about athletes or coaches who have gone down in the history of their sport. But how many others – thousands, probably – have tried and made similar sacrifices? And how many others thought they would make it to the top without making any sacrifices?

That's another choice.

Again, linked to willpower.

Why make so many sacrifices if success is not guaranteed? There is no answer to that.

There's just the doing, in the hope to obtain.

Either that, or we can sit back and do nothing, knowing that many will try and therefore have greater chances. And credit for that goes to them.

Sacrifice cannot be assigned a value, nor can it be gauged. Because everything is always proportional to our needs, preferences and expectations.

How much are our goals worth?

How much are we willing to give to obtain what we want?

How much do our dreams cost?

6) Giving our best, beyond convenience.

I think that giving our best is a basic form of respect and dignity we have for ourselves and for those who believe and have always believed in us. Doing what is just strictly necessary, keeping our talent idling, is an offence to our qualities, to our human nature and to our potential. Whether it's related to sports, to the professional sphere or to our human side.

I believe that this isn't really associated with success; rather with basic ethics, namely, those rules and values that regulate the human behaviour we adopt with ourselves and with others.

Putting all of our effort and our energy into all actions is an ode to the fulfilment of our potential.

Giving our best is not a generic concept. It's not related to games or great missions. It must happen right here, right now. In every step, every strike, every run, every action, every intention. That's the only way to attain the topmost level of excellence, which does justice to our talent, whatever it may be, regardless of the level, the ranking and the visibility of our results.

Sometimes energies fall short. Sometimes the mind cannot help in delivering the best performance, for a number of personal reasons. Sometimes we're not able to give our very best.

It happens.

It's understandable.

We must carry on and head towards the next race, the next match, the next championship. Always moving forward.

But that's beside the point. The point here is not the result. It's the intention.

The intention is everything.

Giving our best means our intention of putting the utmost effort into it, putting our abilities to the best possible use. Here. Now. Whatever they may be. But they must represent our best.

100% of the 70% (if physical or mental conditions are not perfect) is better than half of our full 100%.

There is no thinking of convenience in the intention of giving our best.

There is no efficiency.

There is no energy saving.
It's giving it all. For all.

7) Believing, beyond any expectations.

Believing in ourselves is the first, undisputable and crucial step for reaching any goal. Believing in ourselves and in our abilities must not become blind arrogance, but a positive interpretation of the work we have done so far; it's our trust in what we'll be able to do in the future and in our capacities.

It doesn't mean putting aside self-criticism, the need to constantly improve and grow, or to be aware of the situation. It means to draw the line in a specific moment and believing that, at that point, in that very moment, we can achieve something and give due value to all the hard work and progress made thus far.

Then, we might win it or bin it…

And tomorrow?

It is another day.

Believing that something may happen in a certain way, in terms of visualisation too, is a fundamental step for making it so. Many athletes visualise the result. They picture where the ball from that corner kick will land, where the next pass will go, where they'll be at the finish line. When it happens, they will be ready. At work and in life, believing, being self-confident, trusting other people, imagining and picturing what must happen, based on our expectations, will materialise and realise that opportunity.

How can we believe? Who knows for certain?

It seems reasonable to think that believing is part of our nature, but it's something that can also be trained, by practicing our abilities, which in turn boosts our self-confidence.

But regardless of the professional preparation level, or the number of repetitions of the sporting exercise, believing in ourselves will always have an instinctive element: we must throw our heart over the fence. We also need a bit of recklessness and a dash of arrogance, not versus others but versus our own means.

Believing is much more than having faith in our dreams or in the unknown.

Believing means fulfilling what we have strived for, materialising all our sweat and toil, all the abilities and skills we have developed over time and all the desire built up by doing what we love doing.

We are facing our current worth, which is not unknown to us, for we are the ones who created and fostered it.

It is us, facing the very best of us.

8) Discipline, beyond any excuse or exception.

Wanting to win is surely important. It's something we basically all share. Sure, some may attach more value to it than others, some don't approach victory with the same kind of feelings, but I'd say it's rare for someone to be totally aloof when it comes to victory or defeat. What is even more rare, complicated, and surely more tiring, is the will to prepare to win. Because it requires discipline. A word that sounds like a punishment for those who are hardly willing to make sacrifices and work hard.

Because it's human – very human – to follow the force of gravity. Namely, the path that requires less effort.

But we need discipline to stay the course. Whether we're facing headwinds or being favoured by tailwinds makes no difference. Attention, dedication and confidence are needed, on top of individual skills.

Discipline helps us stay focused, stick to schedules and not give in to distractions that may lead us astray. Discipline is our capacity to uphold our commitment, even when motivation is lacking, regardless of the reason.

Because sometimes we do lack motivation. It happens to everyone.

Discipline entails following a routine, respecting training schedules and staying focused on goals, even in the toughest days.

There is a way to ensure self-discipline: making sure there are no alternatives.

If a shortcut road is closed and we must go around the entire block, then we'll just go around the block. Why? Because the shortcut is closed. Period. We don't like the idea, but we'll have to stick to it.

There is no alternative.

If there's school today, then we must go to school. I can still remember what my son asked me on his second day of primary school: "Should I go to school, even today?"

Yes. Even today. And every day for the next twelve years at least. Then, we'll see.

Period.

Easy enough.

I remember he once asked me the same question on a day when it was snowing heavily, and we were getting him ready for the skiing lessons. I caught the eye of my wife, the best gift I have ever received, hesitated a millisecond and then we said: "Yes. Obviously. It's normal. Every day".

He came back soaking wet.

He survived. And I'm sure we didn't violate any human rights.

In the big picture, both him and our daughter, when they reached the age of seven, had already progressed to the highest ski level, and we could all ski together, anywhere, in any condition. It wasn't about raising a new super champion; it was just about doing, in an orderly and disciplined fashion, what had to be done to complete the round of skiing lessons. The goal? Not winning the ski championship but skiing all together. Something that we like a lot and unites us as a family.

When we do not look for excuses or alternatives, and we don't look for the exception to the rule, it is a lot easier to be disciplined.

Period.

Quite simply, we must not think to the negative side of things, but trust in the process.

Then again, who could ever rationally think it's pleasant to wake up at 6:00 am and go running for 10 kilometres? Lucky sunrise runners… I know just a few of them… Before we can think of a reason not to go, they're already on the street, running. Actually, they've already run one or two kilometres.

Instead of thinking why we shouldn't go, we just say yes and move on. That's it.

Excuses and exceptions don't help us trust the process, nor the development of a regular commitment, that must be upheld and remain solid over time.

Then there's another problem. When must we draw a line to exceptions? Every exception, like a matryoshka doll, contains another one, and each one shall be justified by some sort of reason, and every time the line to be drawn moves further away… Because we can always find a good reason not to do what we don't feel like doing, even if it's the right thing to do.

So, where do we stop? When? Why?

When do we stop shifting further down the line of what is necessary, acceptable or insufficient?

There are no limits to exceptions. The reason why one exception exists is the reason why an exception to it will exist too, and that's already two exceptions, and so on. By making these exceptions, we have lowered the standard and the limit of acceptance. And this generates one consequence only, which is lowering the level, owing to many reasons (all of which are sound), many excuses (all of which are reasonable) and many exceptions (all of which are clearly justified). But in the meantime, the line has moved further down… and the level keeps falling.

How much are we willing to lose for an easy excuse that creates a crack in our motivations, preventing us from doing what we must to fulfil our potential?

9) Determination, beyond any doubt.

As all athletes have said, talent can only take us so far. It's determination that takes us to ever higher performance levels. It's determination that takes us to the finish line.

While victory is tangible once the result has been achieved (whatever it may be in connection with the end goal), it's the journey or the process that has taken us thus far that makes the difference in maximising our probability of success. And in this journey, all the points we have mentioned so far, from 1 to 9, require continuous, constant, incessant determination.

Determination is born from our convictions and compels us to not surrender, even – and especially – when the going gets tough, when doubts turn into lack of faith. There's a moment when some might surrender… and when some carry on. Determination allows us to face adversities and challenges with an unwavering confidence, never letting any difficulty drag us down.

It doesn't mean denying adversities are there. Quite the contrary. Being determined means having the utmost awareness of reality and of the situation, and of the possible implications that will come about at the end of the journey, if we complete it.

Aside from understanding the specific situation and being very realistic, it is possible to catalyse determination by breaking down the problems or the journey into segments or stages that can be tackled and overcome.

By advancing one step at a time, we will go very far.

And it is far more motivating, and easier, to get one thing done every day, rather than waiting weeks to complete the whole lot. It's like climbing a mountain. Every step, every kilometre, every day is a success.

One goal at a time.

One training session at a time.

One repetition at a time.

It is therefore crucial to break down the problem (which cannot be solved in its entirety) or the goal (unachievable in one fell swoop) into aggregable or attainable parts. Each part confirms our abilities, rewards our efforts and testifies a little but constant success. Advancing one step at a time, one metre at a time, is something that will take us very far. Every single step is an advancement and consolidates our motivation and our conviction, for each one of those metres is a conquest, an achieved result. And this gradually strengthens a bit our self-esteem, triggering a positive spiral.

Vice-versa, determination fades away when we aim for a goal that is too large to be taken on all at once.

In this very moment, the book you're reading consists of thirty-three thousand seven hundred and twenty-three words. My 13-year-old son, who has just walked by, noticed this figure, which appears in the bottom left corner of the Word document page. He told me he has never written so many words in his life. I'm pretty sure that's the case, considering the time he spends kicking a ball instead of using a pen!

Anyway, whatever the overall figure may be, these words were written one at a time. One paragraph at a time, one chapter at a time. One day at a time. In just over one year.

The same concept goes for a mountaineer, a marathon runner, a tennis player or a swimmer. It also goes for a civil engineer who must build a skyscraper, one floor at a time. Every floor will be an achievement. A success that has been earned.

Allow me to quote a famous saying, which also gives me the opportunity to flaunt a personal passion of mine: "Rome was not built in a day". It might seem obvious, but it's very true.

And while we're in Rome, I may add "Gutta cavat lapidem" (Lucretius), namely, "The drops that hollows out the stone".

That's right.

One drop at a time.

10) Constant, continuous improvement.

Constant improvement is an endless process that converts today's potential into tomorrow's reality, transforming desire into excellence. It's the secret to growing and advancing. Every single day, we must be better than yesterday. Stronger, faster, more skilled than yesterday.

Because what matters is today.

Not yesterday.

Tomorrow… we'll see.

Constant improvement is the key to long-term success. Athletes must be committed to constant, daily growth, perfecting their skills and pushing themselves beyond their limits. Every single day offers a new opportunity to be a little better than the day before, and this constant process of perfecting oneself is what builds a champion.

In work, and in life, improvement requires observation, curiosity, study, exercise and, above all, self-criticism, which allows us to generate that healthy tension that stimulates growth. Difference in potential creates an electric current. It's physics. Electromagnetism. Life is actually somewhat similar to this principle of physics: where there is a gap, a force is generated; a force that stimulates improvement, so as to bridge that gap.

There is no end to improvement.

Every evening, it takes me some twenty, twenty-five minutes to drive from the office to my home. I never turn the radio on in the car… I just listen to a commentary, my own thoughts of the day. What I saw, what I heard, what I did wrong, what I learnt, what I understood, what I haven't understood, what I should have done differently, what I will do differently, what I must always do, what I will never do.

It helps me. It has helped me over the years. Because repeating this beneficial habit every day, every week, every month, every year brings about a whole lot of thoughts, which have brought about some sort of change. It's a simple, obvious habit, which may even be taken for granted. Still, it's very powerful.

But there is more. It's astonishing to think about what we can learn from so many people, from so many opportunities, at any time, on any given day. Every single interaction can produce unique food for thought. Every single person we observe at a meeting can provide us with unique thoughts. Because everyone is good at at least one thing. Some are good at several things. So, let's multiply this by the number of our colleagues who we interact with, every day, every month, every year. And now let's add up everything we can learn, constantly.

It's not just a matter of training. It's about observing. My "things I have learnt today" list is always open. It's always growing longer. It's incredibly long. Never completed.

Something else that I find interesting is from whom we can learn. At first, when we start in our profession and we're at the base of the pyramid, 99% of interactions occur with peers or superiors, because the entire organisation is above us. Hence, learning happens by looking up and absorbing from our superiors – quite intuitively.

Then, over time, the relationship begins to change. When we're halfway up the pyramid, half of it is above us, the other half is below… and, eventually, we move up, higher and higher, and there's not much to be seen by looking up.

By that stage, either nothing more can be learnt, or we might think we have learnt everything. Or we can look down and listen to the rest of the organisation, which is now below us. But no matter we look, it will surely offer some valuable food for thought.

Because we can always learn something from everyone. A lot can be learnt from our people.

As we walk our path, it is important to understand who we should learn from, and when. It is important to know how to rethink our ability to learn. If we don't do that… we'll simply stop.

The last aspect is about mentorship.

It's hard to find our way without objective, interested but detached guidance.

In my path, I was lucky enough to have several colleagues or bosses who, after our direct relationship changed, kept showing genuine interest in me, and had the innate gift of interpreting emotions without losing sight of their proper dimension. There's at least six of them, all very different. I greatly benefitted from their assessment of events, from their objectiveness and their measure.

Passion, motivation, willpower and determination can only come from the inside.

But the quality of external evaluation, weighting and judgement has no equal.

11) Resilience, beyond any difficulty.

There will be defeats.

Many.

Some will be deserved, so congratulations to our opponents.

Some will not be deserved.

C'est la vie. That's life.

There will be falls. Some will be painful. Some will leave a mark. Some a scar.

Life puts us to the test, constantly.

Technically speaking, resilience is a deformed material's capacity to return to its initial condition, or its ability to absorb a shock without breaking and losing its function. From our standpoint it has a similar meaning: the ability to get back on our feet after every fall, absorbing the shock, continuing to fight, converting adversities into growth opportunities, overcoming difficult periods, defeats and injuries and coming back, stronger than ever.

Resilient athletes can face failures, learn from mistakes and strengthen, day after day, their ability to pursue their own path.

Similarly, we – the athletes of life – must react to personal and professional disappointments. We will suffer our own injuries along the way. We will make our mistakes and must accept the consequences. Sometimes we will face injustice or receive uncalled-for or specious criticisms. Sometimes we will totally deserve to be criticised.

That's reality. It cannot be changed.

Acknowledging that these situations cannot be avoided is fundamental for taking the next step, that is, deciding that we can always do something about it.

Transforming a crisis into change, change into improvement, improvement into results, results into success.

How can that be done?

We must collect our thoughts positively, along with our plans, our life and our habits, to face negative events. Because stopping is not an option. We can only adapt.

Mahatma Gandhi once said: "Life is not about waiting for the storm to pass, it's about learning to dance in the rain". Our external locus would tell us there's nothing we can do about it; we cannot control storms. But our internal locus, defined by Gandhi's quote, urges us not to be overwhelmed, to live intensively, despite the storm. Actually, the storm can be an opportunity to learn to dance…

Objectively and honestly picturing the situation is paramount: we cannot turn a blind eye to reality. It's not about dodging it; it's about knowing it. So that it may be tackled better.

So, while being aware of the situation, it is vital to have a clear understanding of our human and professional qualities. These assets are the foundations from which we must rise again, projecting a positive image of ourselves. Knowing, recalling and writing down our qualities helps. The same goes for our limits.

With the utmost confidence in our strengths, we can get going again, setting simple, clear and attainable goals. Once again, one step at a time.

My boss's boss once sent me a private email, ending it with the following words: "Always forward, with confidence". A simple, straightforward and powerful line. I can still remember it, after many years. I probably will never forget it, considering the context it fell into – one of the most complicated phases of my professional career. With hindsight, I now realise that while that was indeed a delicate context, the best was yet to come… so yes, it worked. Extremely well.

An aphorism ascribed to several authors, including Peter Schultz, which I like to quote during my working groups, is the following: "We cannot decide to direct the wind, but we can always adjust the sails to reach our destination". This single ability enables a boat to sail, regardless of the wind's direction, hence upwind too.

It can be linked to another line, extremely realistic (and rather blunt), ascribed to Edward Gibbon: "The winds and the waves are always on the side of the ablest navigators". We can complain, find excuses, justifications and reasons, but the winner is always right. Finally, remaining amid the waves, let me quote Seneca the Elder: "There is no favourable wind for the sailor who doesn't know where to go". As if to say: we must always have clear, straightforward ideas in mind. Or we won't be able to create the ideal conditions that underlie true success.

We need a proper understanding of reality, as well as full confidence in our ability to shape it through our own efforts.

That's how we develop resilience and optimism.

That's how we adapt to the circumstances, how we get back on our feet after falling.

That's how we keep on going.

Always forward.

With confidence.

Essentially, there are many elements that factor into the equation for maximising our potential. Whether it's our potential related to sports, work or our personal sphere. For new generations too, there are some universal truths that transcend time and culture, despite the change in tools, habits, technologies and preferences. These truths are proven by highly successful champions and unite us all, in sports, at work and in everyday life, whatever our goals may be.

We must be passionate, brave and determined.

We must keep on improving, making sacrifices and giving our very best.

We must believe in ourselves and be disciplined, intentionally choosing our own path and staying the course, with no exceptions.

We must face all challenges with resilience, confidence and persistence.

Dreams can come true.

The future is totally in our hands.

Don't believe those who place all sources of frustration on the outside or tell us that we have fallen victim to unfortunate, random and uncontrollable events.

We are our own future.

Believing in ourselves and guiding our own future with confidence and courage through a non-negotiable commitment – which may never be betrayed in exchange for fleeting and evanescent rewards – is something that carries a value which cannot be measured. And we shape our way based on this very set of values.

The world is ready to find out what we're capable of.

Let's not limit ourselves.

There are no limits.

I have always loved mathematics.

And the value it gives to infinity.

∞.

BONUS QUESTIONS AND ANSWERS

WHEN DID YOU REALIZE THAT YOU WOULD BECOME SOMEONE WHO WOULD WIN IN SPORTS?

RONALDINHO
Every time I played, I saw the joy and smiles of the people around me.

LANCE BRAUMAN
As a coach I have always been motivated to make my athletes successful. I think my mission is to lead others to success; So, there is no time when I ever felt like I "made it," because my role is to create success for others.

NATALIA GUTLIER
When I decided to become a professional and dedicate all of myself, all my commitment and my energy to that goal. Both when I started my career in tennis and when I decided a few years later to play footvolley and teqball at a professional level. I didn't want to be just an athlete, but I wanted to devote myself completely to making the best of myself.

XAVI
Maybe the first time was when I joined La Masia at the age of eleven. Barcelona instills that winning gene, demands and teaches you to seek the excellence I mentioned earlier. A little later, I reinforced this mentality when I saw that with our generation, we were able to win, with the Spanish youth national team or with the Under-21s, against countries like Italy, Germany, Brazil and other national teams that we have always admired. At the elite level, the push that made us believe we could beat anyone came from Luis Aragonés in the national team; he made us believe in ourselves and cultivated the winning mentality, laying the foundations for that incredible cycle. Then, at Barça, with Pep Guardiola and that unique generation we had, it was impossible not to

have that winning mentality, because of the prestige of the club and because with that team we had to try to win everything.

KAKÁ

There is not a single time in your professional and personal life when you set goals and strive to reach them. Every moment can be an achievement and a victory. The sum of all this takes you to a high level, but every step and every moment counts.

STAN SMITH

It was a gradual thing. I had success as a junior, then in college. I won the Junior National Championships, then I won the NCAA. But the moment that really made a difference to the highest level was when I won the first Pepsi-Cola Masters in Tokyo in 1970, which is now one of the last tournaments on the ATP Tour 500. I was really impressed when Rosewall was asked who the favorites were for the tournament, and he said I was the favorite or one of the favorites. And hearing him say it really made a difference. The other thing that happened to me shortly before was the defeat against Gonzalez, who was ten years older than me, in the quarterfinals of the Wembley indoor tournament, before Stockholm and before the Masters. Jack Kramer, whom I had enormous respect for because he was considered by many to be the father of professional tennis, said to me: "Look, boy," he always called you boy, "you're really playing well, don't let that put you off." So, after losing to Gonzalez in the final, I won the doubles, and then the singles and doubles in Stockholm and then the singles and doubles at the Masters. And so, those words of encouragement made a big difference. So that was the turning point, I think, to decide if I could really be number one in the world.

FELIPE SCOLARI

In sport you always have to win. When I won the first title it was wonderful, but in the next competition I had to do it again. It is always like that. Success and success, year after year. I have won several titles in national leagues and international competitions, but I must keep winning if I continue as a coach.

IAN THORPE

I became world champion when I had just turned fifteen. Strangely before that I thought I was a talented young swimmer, but I didn't know if I would be able to reach the top in my sport... And then it happened. When it happened, I didn't know if it would ever happen again; However, a year later I had broken several world records and, at seventeen, I realized what was my childhood dream, which was to become an Olympic champion.

ROBERTO MANCINI

At first, I knew I had qualities. But then, especially the first years in Bologna, I saw many young people who had great qualities but who didn't make it. So, I realized that even quality and talent were not enough. Then after a few years I realized that I could have a life full of satisfaction at a sporting level, but to stay at certain levels it was necessary to work hard and seriously with great continuity.

WHAT'S YOUR GREATEST FEAR?

RONALDINHO
The suffering from losing someone I love.

LANCA BRAUMAN
To become one of those people who lose their passion and love for what they do.

NATALIA GUTLIER
There are two! One is to stop getting better at what I do. The other is not being healthy enough to do so.

XAVI
My main fear is that something bad could happen to my children. My wish is that they grow up healthy and in a stable and safe environment. I think that, like any parent, when you have children, they become your main concern.

KAKÁ
When you have a family, your biggest fear is always related to it. But when you dedicate yourself and have faith, any fear, whether in your personal or professional life, also becomes a force to overcome challenges.

STAN SMITH
Not being able to train hard and not playing at competitive levels. Those were truly my biggest fears. Then going to the dentist was not one of my favorite things… and playing Borg on the clay was like going to the dentist: not a great experience

FELIPE SCOLARI

In everyday life I have no particular fears.

ROBERTO MANCINI

I don't have great fears, because I think sport is made up of victories and defeats. So, I think the best thing is to stay in the game as long as possible, because then the time comes when you can't do it anymore; therefore, being able to stay at high levels is important.

SEX AND SPORT – RETREAT OR NOT?

ALESSANDRO DEL PIERO

Sexual activity can be part of a balanced life, but during training or retreats the focus is often on discipline and minimizing distractions, so abstinence can be expected.

RONALDINHO

Everyone can make their own choice. Mine has always been very clear...

NATALIA GUTLIER

I think it can provide an overall sense of relaxation. Relieving the tension and the pressure.

RIVALDO

I think there is a right time for everything.

XAVI

I believe that in sport, as in life, it is better to rely on common sense and spontaneity. Sex is part of our lives, so we know when and how to practice it. I don't think restrictions are necessarily positive.

KAKÁ

This is a theme that has a different importance for each person. There is no rule. With maturity and professionalism, everyone must deal with this topic in a healthy way.

FELIPE SCOLARI

Whether we are talking about concentration, training camp or pre-season, those are moments in which the priority is to form a group and prepare. Therefore, no other activities are planned at those times.

ROBERTO MANCINI

I don't know, today there are many games and therefore we tend to make fewer withdrawals, and the games are also less tiring. But I don't think it's a problem, I don't think it ever was.

WHO IS THE CHAMPION OF THE CENTURY? WHY?

ALESSANDRO DEL PIERO
This is subjective and depends on the sport. Champions are those who not only excel in their field but also manage to inspire others and make a positive impact on the sport.

RONALDINHO
There is no single one, as they all have merits, regardless of the size or relative relevance of their results. In football, Pelé will always be our eternal idol and Maradona a friend we miss so much.

LANCE BRAUMAN
Jesse Owens: his achievements have been greater than the sport itself.

WAYDE VAN NIEKERK
In the thirty years that I have lived, my champion of this century would be Jürgen Klopp. A somewhat biased answer, as I am a big Liverpool fan, but he is also a very inspirational person. If I look at the people who have come to success by taking a team from a fighting position to a victorious one and becoming a champion by writing history, then I think Jürgen Klopp has been a really great example in every single team he has coached.

NATALIA GUTLIER
I have been very inspired by the carriers of Federer and Serena Williams! I think they are two icons of sport who have broken many records on top of playing exceptionally.

XAVI

If we refer to football, to me, without any doubt, Lionel Messi. I believe the best player in history.

KAKA

This can be very subjective. I prefer to keep a certain distance from discussing the careers of others. I believe that these disputes about who was the best end up impoverishing the debate. Many have had great results and successes.

STAN SMITH

The six boys Laver, Borg, Stan Smith, Nadal, Djokovic and Federer. Not necessarily in that order. I would like to put Federer at the top because I think there is a difference between a winner and a champion. A winner is one who statistically has done everything, perhaps at his best. The champion is the one who won and also represented the game, he was an ambassador for it. So, I would look at Federer in this regard. In the women's game, Serena, Steffi and Margaret are perhaps the top three (Williams, Graf and Smith Court).

FELIPE SCOLARI

If the question relates to the 21st century then I believe it's Manchester City.

IAN THORPE

Michael Phelps is undoubtedly the champion of the century.

ROBERTO MANCINI

I don't know. Honestly, there are so many in all sports, from football, basketball, boxing, tennis, skiing, athletics. It is really very difficult to say one!

IF YOU WERE ANOTHER ATHLETE, WHO WOULD YOU LIKE TO BE AND WHY?

RONALDINHO
I am very happy with who I am, and I admire the achievements of many other athletes. It is impossible to list in one person everything I admire about many other sportsmen.

WAYDE VAN NIEKERK
Probably Cristiano Ronaldo. I really love his passion and his desire to want to win and to want to be the best. And his discipline, his sacrifice and his ability to work very hard. He appears as a very passionate and decisive person, and these are qualities that I would have really liked to add to who I am as an athlete, but it's one of the hardest things to implement.

NATALIA GUTLIER
I think that Marta (Brazilian football player) is, without any doubt, an icon and source of inspiration given what she represents as an athlete and for her record in a sport still predominantly male.

XAVI
I think that I would probably choose Michael Jordan.

KAKA
There is no one I would like to be like, we all had successes and made mistakes and everyone who has reached a high level has set great examples. I like to analyze several of them and every time I have the opportunity to meet them, I ask them to tell me how each one got there.

STAN SMITH

Basketball was my first love, but now I enjoy playing golf. You know, it's more like tennis. I would probably play golf because it's one-on-one. I really like Scheffler. I also admire Tom Brady, because he's probably the one who came closest to reaching his potential. It is the closest to one hundred percent for results and longevity.

FELIPE SCOLARI

I am happy and grateful for my career as a defender and coach.

ROBERTO MANCINI

I have been extremely happy to play football because it has always been the sport that I have been most passionate about, even if I like them all. I would have liked to play an individual sport, because not being able to count on the contribution of your teammates you have to give much more.

ATHLETES' BIOGRAPHIES

TIGIST ASSEFA
Born in Ethiopia in 1996, she is one of the most remarkable marathon runners of the modern era, known for her extraordinary progression from middle-distance track athlete to world-record-breaking marathoner.
Originally an 800 m specialist who represented Ethiopia at the 2016 Rio Olympics, Tigist transitioned to road racing, where she rapidly became a dominant force. In her marathon career, she has achieved historic milestones, including:
- 3 World Marathon Majors (Berlin 2 times, London)
- Silver Olympic medal and Vice World Champion
- First women under 2:14, 2:13 and 2:12
- 2023 World Athlete of the year.

Her 2:11:53 marathon world record set in Berlin 2023 stands as the fastest women's marathon time ever recorded, beating the previous record by around 2 minutes, redefining what is considered possible in women's distance running and inspiring a new generation of athletes worldwide.

CLAUDIO BERARDELLI
One of the most successful and influential endurance coaches in modern athletics. Italian, he has guided numerous Olympic, World, and

Major Marathon champions over the past two decades, shaping the rise of Kenyan middle- and long-distance dominance across track and road running.

Among the athletes he has coached are Olympic champions, world record holders, and winners of the world's most prestigious marathons — including Martin Lel, Nancy Langat, Janeth Jepkosgei, Alfred Kirwa Yego, Priscah Jeptoo, Evans Chebet, Benson Kipruto, Amos Kipruto, Emmanuel Wanyonyi, Sabastian Sawe.

He boasts:

- 6 Olympic medals (including 3 golds)
- 10 World Championship gold medals
- 10 World Marathon Major victories (London, Boston, New York, Chicago, Tokyo)
- 6 World Half Marathon and Road Running titles
- More than 25 podium finishes in World Marathon Majors
- Over 20 athletes ranked #1 in their event globally

Founder and head coach of the 2RunningClub, based in Kapsabet, Kenya, Claudio has built one of the world's most respected training environments — a place where champions are developed through precision, patience, and human connection. His legacy continues to shape the future of middle- and long-distance running worldwide.

USAIN BOLT

Born in Sherwood Content (Jamaica) in 1986, world record holder in the 100m, 200m and 4x100m relay, he is considered to be the greatest sprinter of all time and is the only athlete in history to have won the gold medal in the 100m and 200m in three consecutive editions of the Olympic Games, as well as in three different editions of the world championships. He also held the world records for the 200m in the under-20 and under-18 categories until 2021.

In his career:

- He won 8 Olympic golds; 11 world championships golds, 2 silvers, 1 bronze
- He holds the world records in the 100m, 200m and 4x100m relay.
- He has been elected as the world athlete of the year 6 times.

He has broken the world record on 8 occasions, in the 100m, 200m, and 4x100m.

LANCE BRAUMAN

One of the most successful coaches in the history of athletics. American, he has coached many of the most successful athletes of the last 20 years, including world record holders, Olympic gold medalists and world and national record holders: from Noah Lyles to Wayde van Niekerk, Jereem Richards, Shaunae Miller Uibo, Tyson Gay, Gina Lückenkemper.

He boasts

- 8 Olympic medals including 6 gold medals
- 13 World Championship Gold Medals
- 20 Diamond League Championships
- 3 Commonwealth Championships
- 18 times #1 world ranking in the discipline

Lance founded Pure Athletics in 2007, based in Clermont, Florida, USA.

ALESSANDRO DEL PIERO

Born in Conegliano in 1974, he is considered one of the best Italian players of all time and among the strongest in the world of his generation. Attacking midfielder or second striker, gifted with a superb technique, and great dribbling, running and ball-control. A specialist in set pieces, he inspired an entire generation with his "Del Piero shots".

A world champion, he is the top scorer in history for Juventus and the player with the most appearances. He is the Italian player with the most goals from free kicks in all competitions, the fourth best scorer in the history of the Italian national team, and the tenth best scorer in the history of the Serie A. He has scored 359 goals in 897 matches, played at an average of about 1 goal every two matches and is the only Italian player to have scored a brace at the Santiago Bernabeu, celebrated with a standing ovation as he left the pitch.

Among other titles he has won:
- 6 national championships, 1 Italian Cup, 4 Italian Super Cups.
- 1 UEFA Champions League, 1 Intercontinental Cup, 1 UEFA Cup
- 2-time top scorer in the Champions League
- 1 World Cup

He played 120 games for the Italian national team, 91 of which were for the senior national team, scoring a total of 43 goals.

SERGIO GARCIA FERNÀNDEZ

Born in Castellon de la Plana in 1980, he was the first golfer to win both the Masters and The Players Championship and is the golfer who has achieved the most points in the history of the Ryder Cup, representing Europe in 10 editions. He has won 11 tournaments on the PGA tour and 16 on the European tour and was crowned world team champion with Spain. His titles include:
- 1 Masters
- 6 Ryder Cups with the highest number of points in the history of the Ryder Cup
- 1 players Championship
- 11 victories in PGA Tour tournaments
- 16 DP World Tour victories
- 1 Golf World Cup
- Byron Nelson Award, Rookie of the year, Vardon Trophy

NATALIA GUTLIER

Born in Rio de Janeiro in 1987, she began her professional sports career as a tennis player, winning 5 ITF titles, before moving on to emerging football sports such as footvolley and teqball, in which she won 3 world championships.

- Women's World Champion Teqball Singles
- World Champion Teqball Mixed Doubles
- World Champion Footvolley
- "Reina de la Playa" title in world footvolley for two consecutive years.

GRANT HOLLOWAY

Born in Chesapeake in 1997, he is probably already the best 60m and 100m hurdles specialist in history, and already one of the most titled ever. Already an Olympic champion, 3-time world champion, indoor world champion, undefeated in the 60m indoor hurdles (up to today: 94 consecutive wins) and world record holder. He has the second fastest time ever in the 110m hurdles, he has run the most races in history (12 times) under 13 sec. in the 110m hurdles and holds the NCAA record.

His successes include:
- 1 Olympic gold and 1 Olympic silver
- 3-time world champion.
- 2-time world champion 60m indoor hurdles. World record 60m indoor hurdles.
- 1 Diamond League
- NCAA record in the 110m hurdles and 4x100m.

PERES JEPCHIRCHIR

Born in Kenya in 1993, she is one of the most successful marathon runners in the history of world athletics, being also the first woman to have won both a world marathon major and an Olympic gold.

In her 8-year career, she has won 14 of the 21 international races in which she has participated. Among others she has won:
- 3 world half marathon championships
- 1 world marathon championships
- 1 Olympic gold
- 4 world marathon majors (Boston, NYC, London 2 times)
- Multiple world records in both half marathon and marathon.

Peres has broken the world record for the half marathon 3 times and currently holds the world record for the marathon (women only) set in London in 2024. Renowned for her tactical intelligence, unshakable confidence, and devastating finishing, Peres has redefined the art of racing — setting a new benchmark for strategic brilliance and competitive excellence in women's distance running.

JACKIE JOYNER-KERSEE

Born in St. Louis in 1962, she is one of the greatest athletes of all time. Her world record in the heptathlon has stood for 37 years, and she holds all six of the best world performances of all time and has broken the Olympic record in the long jump. 3-time Olympic champion, 4-time World champion, and Pan American Games champion. During college at UCLA as a basketball player she scored over 1000 points and is listed in the 15 best players in UCLA history. Her achievements include:
- World record in the heptathlon, which has stood since 1988, and all six of the best world performances in history.
- Olympic record in the long jump
- 3 Olympic golds
- 4 World golds
- World Athlete of the Year.

Sports Illustrated named Jackie the best female athlete of the 20th century.

KAKÀ

Born in 1982 in Gama, Ricardo Izecson dos Santos leite, Kakà is considered one of the greatest Brazilian players in history. Golden Ball and world champion, equipped with excellent technique, he was a complete attacking midfielder with great vision of the game. He was known for his dribbling, progression with the ball at his feet and shooting from distance. His many trophies include:
- Golden Ball. FIFA world player.
- 2 national championships, one cup and two super cups in Italy and Spain.
- 1 UEFA Champions League, 1 UEFA Super Cup, 1 Club World Cup
- 1 World Cup, 2 Confederation Cups.

He scored 209 goals in 659 appearances as a professional between Sao Paulo, Milan, Real Madrid and Orlando City in his 16 year career and 34 goals in 100 appearances for the national team. Kaka is the top Brazilian scorer in the history of the Champions League with 28 goals.

NOAH LYLES

Born in Gainesville, Florida in 1997, Noah is one of the most successful 100m and 200m sprinters in the history of American and world athletics. 6-time world champion, Olympic champion, Diamond League Champion, he is known for his athletic performance but also for his strong personality and creative abilities. His achievements include:
- 1 Olympic gold in the 100m, 2 bronze medals
- 6-time world champion, and 2-time U20 world champion
- 5-time Diamond League champion
- 6-time American national track champion.
- World Athlete of the year 2023
- American record in the 200m (19:31) and third fastest time in the history of the 200m

In addition to his success on the track, Noah is a passionate advocate for freedom of personal expression, fusing his love of fashion, anime and music to inspire a new generation of athletes and fans.

ROBERTO MANCINI

Born in Jesi in 1964, he is considered one of the best attacking midfielders in the history of Italian football and one of the most successful Italian coaches in the world. After making his debut in Serie A at the age of 16, he scored 204 goals in 739 career games at club level and made 62 appearances for the national team, scoring 13 goals. As a player he won:
- 2 Italian championships,6 Italian cups and 2 Italian super-cups
- 2 UEFA cups, 2 cup winners' cups

As a coach he collected:
- 3 Italian championships, 4 Italian cups, 2 Italian super-cups
- 1 Premier League, 1 FA cup, 1 Community Shield, 1 Turkish cup
- 1 European championship with the Italian national team.
- Named coach of the year by Globe Soccer award and World Soccer

At club level he won 277 out of 507 matches with an average win percentage of 54%. Roberto won more than 28 titles in his career both as a player and as a coach, winning wherever he played or coached. He has broken several records:
- Most Italian Cups won as a player (6), most appearances (120) and most Italian Cups won as a coach (4)
- 3 consecutive Serie A titles won with Inter, setting a record for the club.
- With Manchester City he won the Premier League after 44 years and the FA Cup, the first major trophy for the club after 35 years

- 37 games without defeat with the Italian national team, 9 consecutive victories, qualification for Euro 2020 with all victories in the group.

STAN SMITH

Born in Pasadena in 1946, he is the eighth most titled tennis player in history and considered one of the 20 best ever. He was number 1 in the world, he obtained 64 titles, winning 779 of the 1084 matches he played as a professional (72%). Among other titles, he boasts:
- 7 Davis Cups
- 4 grand slams (2 singles, 2 doubles)
- 2 Tour Finals

Through the partnership with Adidas that accompanied him as a technical sponsor throughout Stan Smith's career both as a player and as a coach, the previous "Haillet" was renamed, and became "Stan Smith" in 1978

SHAUNAE MILLER-UIBO

Born in Nassau in 1994, she is one of the most titled sprinters in the history of the women's 400m: World, Olympic, indoor, outdoor and both senior and junior champion. She has won all possible competitions at national, world and Olympic level both as a Junior and as a senior. Her titles include:
- 12 national titles
- 2 Olympic golds
- 4 Diamond Leagues
- World champion. Indoor world champion. U20 and U18 world champion.
- Commonwealth Games Champion
- 3-time Continental Cup Champion
- World record in 200m straight and 150m straight

RONALDINHO

Ronaldo de Assis Moreira, born in Porto Alegre in 1980, is recognized as one of the best players in the history of football, thanks to an extraordinary technique and a unique flair. Neymar says of him: "He was a genius, the greatest showman of football". He scored 266 goals in 699 appearances as a professional between Gremio, Paris Saint-Germain, Barcelona, Milan, Flamengo, Atletico Mineiro, Queretaro and Fluminense in his 17 year career and 62 goals in 154 appearances for the national team. He has won, among other things:
- 1 Ballon d'Or, 2 FIFA World Players
- 2 national championships, 2 Spanish Super Cups
- 1 UEFA Champions League, 1 Copa Libertadores, 1 Recopa Sudamericana
- 1 World Cup, 1 Confederation Cup, 1 Under 17 World Cup, 1 Olympic bronze.

ARRIGO SACCHI

Born in Fusignano in 1946, he is one of the most successful and innovative coaches in the history of world football. France Football magazine placed him in 3rd place in the list of the 50 best coaches of all time. His Milan from 1987 to 1991 is considered one of the teams that developed the best football in the history of football, combining the application of the zone, defense in line and systematic pressing in midfield, creating a form of total football in which the players had a continuous role in both the offensive and defensive phases. His trophies include:
- 1 Italian championship, 1 Italian super cup.
- 2 Champions Leagues, 2 UEFA Super Cups, 2 Intercontinental Cups
- World Cup runner-up.
- World Soccer Coach of the Year

Arrigo Sacchi is the only coach in history to have won the combination of the Champions Cup, UEFA Super Cup and Intercontinental Cup for two consecutive years.

LUIZ FELIPE SCOLARI

Born in Passo Fundo in 1948. World champion and winner of the Confederation Cup with Brazil, he is, together with Marcello Lippi, the only coach in history to have won the top international club competition in two different continents (Asia and America).

In his career he has won:
- 1 World Cup, 1 Confederations Cup with Brazil, 1 Gulf National Cup. European Championships Runner-Up with Portugal.
- 2 Brazilian Championships, 4 Brazilian Cups, in 3 different teams.
- 1 AFC Champions League, 2 Copa Libertadores, 1 Recopa Sudamericana,
- 1 Kuwaiti championship, 1 Kuwait Emir Cup, 3 Chinese championships, 1 Chinese cup, two Chinese Supercups.

As a club coach, he won 551 of 1163 matches played with an average win rate of 49%

COREY SEAGER

Born in Charlotte in 1994, Seager plays for the Texas Rangers and is considered the best shortstop of his generation. Rookie of the Year, MLB All-Star already in his first two seasons in the Major League, NL Championship MVP and World Series MVP. The first left-handed shortstop in MLB history to reach 200 home runs, he also holds the records for the most home runs by a left-handed shortstop in a season, the most doubles in a season by a rookie of the Dodgers and was the first player to obtain the title of MVP of the World Series and NLCS in the same year. Among his successes, he has won:
- 5 All-Star.

- 2 World Series
- 2 World Series MVP, NLCS MVP
- NL Rookie of the Year
- 3 Silver Slugger Awards.

IAN THORPE

Born in Sydney in 1982, he is considered one of the greatest swimmers of all time. He was the youngest Australian athlete, at 14, to represent the country at the Olympic Games and a year later, at 15, he became the youngest individual male world champion in history. At 16, he was the youngest swimmer in history to set a world record, which was followed by 22 others. By the end of his career, he was:

- 5-time Olympic champion with a total of 9 Olympic medals in just 2 Olympic Games.
- 11-time world swimming champion, and 2 times in short course
- A 23 time world record holder
- 4-time World Swimmer of the Year

Ian is one of the greatest swimmers in the history of world swimming and the most titled Australian athlete in history.

WAYDE VAN NIEKERK

Born in Cape Town in 1992, he is the current world record holder in the 400m, as well as the first athlete in history to have run the 100m in less than 10 seconds, the 200m in less than 20 seconds and the 400m in less than 44 seconds. He is the first African athlete to win the world title in the 400m, and his world record in the 400m has been unbeaten for 9 years.

His titles include:

- 400m world record
- 1 Olympic gold medal
- 2 World Championships

- 2 African Championships
- 5 other silver medals in world championships, world relays, commonwealth games, African championships and Universiade.

In 2017, during a charity rugby match, he suffered a serious injury to his knee ligaments, forcing him to undergo reconstruction surgery and a long rehabilitation period, resulting in his absence from competitions for all of 2017 and 2018.

XAVI

Xavier Hernández Creus, born in Terrassa in 1980, is considered one of the strongest midfielders in history. As a playmaker or defensive midfielder, he showed an extraordinary vision of the game, precision in his passes and timing in his movements. He knew how to alternate great ability in dribbling in tight spaces with the search for depth and sudden verticalization.

He dedicated 23 years of his playing career to Barcelona, winning more than 25 trophies, and returning to coach, winning the league and the Spanish Super Cup. He has 190 appearances for the national team (starting from the Under 17s) and 26 goals. He has won, among other accolades:

- 8 national championships, 3 Spanish Cups, 6 Spanish Super Cups
- 4 UEFA Champions Leagues, 2 UEFA Super Cups, 2 Club World Cups
- 1 World Cup, 2 European Championships, 1 Under-20 World Cup, 1 Olympic silver

As a coach he won a championship and a Spanish Super Cup with Barcelona. In Qatar, he won 1 championship and two Cups.

Printed in Dunstable, United Kingdom